Maximising the Impact of Teaching Assistants

Teaching assistants are an integral part of classroom life, yet pioneering research by the authors has shown schools are not making the most of this valued resource. Evidence shows that the more support pupils receive from TAs, the less academic progress they make. Yet the reason for this has little to do with TAs. It is decisions made *about* them by school leaders and teachers that best explain this provocative finding.

The fully updated second edition of this book draws on the experiences of schools that have put this guidance into action via the Maximising the Impact of Teaching Assistants programme. Revised to reflect the latest research evidence and changes within education, including the 2014 SEND Code of Practice, this book will help school leaders and teachers in primary and secondary settings to rethink the role, purpose and contribution of TAs and add real value to what can be achieved in classrooms.

Setting out a field-tested process, structured around a coherent and empirically sound conceptual framework, this book:

- helps school leaders review, reform and re-energise their TA workforce
- provides practical strategies to implement in the classroom
- illustrates key points with new case studies
- provides photocopiable templates and links to online resources to support decision-making and action.

Maximising the Impact of Teaching Assistants provides much-needed and evidence-informed guidance on how to unleash the huge potential of TAs, and is essential reading for all school leaders.

Rob Webster is a researcher at the UCL Institute of Education, London, UK, where he also leads the Maximising the Impact of Teaching Assistants programme. He has previously worked as a teaching assistant in mainstream and special schools.

Anthony Russell was a researcher at the UCL Institute of Education, London, UK, and has previously worked as a teacher, science adviser and Deputy Director of the APU science team at King's College, London, UK.

Peter Blatchford is Professor in Psychology and Education at the UCL Institute of Education, London, UK, and has directed large-scale research programmes on class size, support staff and collaborative group work.

Maximising the Impact of Teaching Assistants

Guidance for school leaders and teachers

Second edition

Rob Webster, Anthony Russell and
Peter Blatchford

Routledge
Taylor & Francis Group

LONDON AND NEW YORK

Second edition published 2016
by Routledge
2 Park Square, Milton Park, Abingdon, Oxon OX14 4RN

and by Routledge
711 Third Avenue, New York, NY 10017

Routledge is an imprint of the Taylor & Francis Group, an informa
business

First edition published 2013 by Routledge

British Library Cataloguing-in-Publication Data
A catalogue record for this book is available from the British Library

Library of Congress Cataloging in Publication Data
A catalog record for this book has been requested

ISBN: 978-1-138-90710-2 (hbk)
ISBN: 978-1-138-90711-9 (pbk)
ISBN: 978-1-315-69516-7 (ebk)

Typeset in Sabon
by Saxon Graphics Ltd, Derby

Contents

Acknowledgements

Throughout this book we have reflected the 'real world' experiences of schools with whom we have had the privilege to work since the publication of the first edition in 2013. The second edition has given us the opportunity to supplement the case studies contained in the first edition, which were taken from the Effective Deployment of Teaching Assistants project.

We are grateful to the schools listed below who agreed to let us share their experiences in this book. They include some of the 'early adopters' of the Maximising the Impact of Teaching Assistants programme in London and Essex:

All Saints' CE Primary School, Croydon, South London
Beam County Primary School, Dagenham, Essex
Beauchamps High School, Wickford, Essex
Beech Hill Primary School, Halifax, West Yorkshire
Fairburn Primary School, Fairburn, West Yorkshire
Featherstone High School, Ealing, West London
Great Clacton CE Junior School, Clacton-on-Sea, Essex
Grove Wood Primary School, Rayleigh, Essex
Hadley Learning Community, Telford, Shropshire
Harmans Water Primary School, Bracknell Forest, Berkshire
Haydon School, Hillingdon, West London
Heartlands High School, Haringey, North London
Lexden Springs School, Colchester, Essex
Lincewood Primary School, Langdon Hills, Essex
Little Ealing Primary School, Ealing, West London
Oakthorpe Primary School, Enfield, North London
Pyrgo Primary School, Romford, Essex
St. Andrew's CE Primary School, Brixton, South London
St. Benedict's Catholic College, Colchester, Essex
Swayne Park School, Rayleigh, Essex

We would also like to extend our thanks to the many local authority staff and advisors with whom we have worked to deliver the school improvement programme, which is based on this book, and to the many school leaders, teachers, TAs, trainers and others we have met who have been so complimentary about the first edition.

Finally, we must thank the Esmée Fairbairn Foundation for funding the Effective Deployment of Teaching Assistants project; the work which forms the base of this book.

Acknowledgements

Introduction

This book is a guide to help school leaders and practitioners who want to rethink the use of teaching assistants (TAs). In this introduction, we give the background to the second edition of this book.

The Deployment and Impact of Support Staff (DISS) study

The DISS study (2003–2009) was designed to help fill gaps in knowledge about TAs' deployment and impact. There were two broad aims:

1   To provide an accurate, systematic and representative description of the types of support staff and their characteristics and deployment in schools, and how these changed over time.
2   To analyse the impact of support staff on teachers, teaching and pupil learning, behaviour and academic progress. The study focused on all types of support staff and all pupils.

This was the largest study yet undertaken on support staff and involved a large-scale nationally representative questionnaire survey involving: nearly 18,000 responses from school leaders, support staff and teachers; detailed analysis of the effect of TA support on the academic progress of 8,200 pupils; detailed systematic observations, work pattern diaries and transcripts giving systematic accounts of TAs' activities and interactions; and in-depth case studies. The findings received wide media coverage and, in September 2014, it was named by the British Educational Research Association as one of 40 landmark studies to have had a significant impact on education in the last 40 years. The results are described in full in our book: *Reassessing the Impact of Teaching Assistants* (Blatchford et al. 2012b).

Findings on the impact of TA support on pupils' learning

The DISS project found that the effect of TA support on pupils' academic progress is at variance with the positive views of teachers about their impact. The study assessed the effects of TA support on pupils' academic progress in English, mathematics and science. Two 'waves' (or cohorts) of pupils in seven age groups across the primary and secondary years were tracked from the beginning to the end of the school year. The results were striking. Of the possible 21 results (there were seven age groups and three subjects), 16 were in a negative direction. These results stood, even when accounting for the factors that are known to affect academic progress and the allocation of TA support, such as prior attainment and level of special educational needs (SEN). Importantly, there were no positive effects of TA support for any subject for any year group.

To summarise, pupils receiving the most TA support made less progress than similar pupils who received little or no TA support – even after controlling for factors likely to be related to academic progress and the allocation of TA support (e.g. prior attainment and SEN status).

The DISS results were a 'wake-up call' and they made it clear that urgent action now needs to be taken to address the way TAs are used in schools. In our book *Reassessing the Impact of Teaching Assistants*, we explain that the fault does not lie with individual TAs, but with decisions made about how TAs are used, albeit with the best of intentions, by schools and teachers. We also developed the 'Wider Pedagogical Role' (WPR) model to both summarise findings from the DISS project and to suggest possible explanations for the results on academic progress. The WPR model enables us to interpret the impact of TA support on pupils' academic progress within the wider context of the factors within which TAs work, and over which they have little or no control.

We unpack the WPR model in more detail in Chapter 1. However, it is necessary for what follows in this chapter to say something about its three main components. First, there is the *deployment* of TAs by school leaders and teachers; that is, which pupils TAs are allocated to work with. The DISS project showed that this will typically be individuals and groups of lower-attaining pupils and those with SEN. Deployment also relates to the effects of wider strategic decision-making, and the extent to which the way TAs are used in classrooms is informed by a clear and consistent school-level vision about the role, purpose and contribution. Secondly, there is the *practice* of TAs, which can be thought of as the fine point of deployment. Practice specifically concerns the nature and quality of their interactions with pupils, which we found to be far less academically demanding and much more task-driven, compared with teacher-to-pupil interactions.

Finally, we have the *preparedness* of TAs and teachers, which covers: (i) their training for their respective roles (for teachers, this will influence how they make the most of TAs in their classrooms, and for TAs, training will influence their pedagogical and subject understanding); and (ii) the amount of planning, preparation and debriefing/feedback time available for teachers and TAs, and the quality of the information that flows between them. These factors, working in combination, which govern TAs' employment and deployment, offer the most fruitful answers to questions about the effectiveness of TA support.

On the basis of the findings from the DISS project and our work to conceptualise these findings in terms of the WPR model, we concluded that a fundamental rethink is required in the way TAs are used in order to avoid letting down supported pupils.

The Effective Deployment of Teaching Assistants (EDTA) project

Following the DISS project, we conducted a project funded by the Esmée Fairbairn Foundation in which we worked with schools and teacher and TA pairs in two local authorities in England. This project was invaluable as a way of developing and evaluating alternative ways of using TAs that worked for schools and for pupils, and which dealt with the negative impact of TAs identified in the DISS project. We will describe this project in more detail in the next chapter. The EDTA project was supplemented by extensive discussions with school leaders, teachers and local authority staff with responsibilities for the TA workforce and for pupils with SEN during the numerous in-service training (inset) and consultancy activities that we have undertaken since the publication of the DISS project findings. Our work was also informed by the work of Professor Michael Giangreco of the University of Vermont, USA, and his colleagues, as well as other commentators and researchers.

As a result of this work, it was strongly felt that a book of guidance on the effective deployment of TAs would be extremely helpful to school leaders and class teachers interested in understanding and improving the ways in which they deploy TAs across schools and within classrooms. The outcome was the first edition of this book, published in 2013.

The Maximising the Impact of Teaching Assistants (MITA) programme

The first edition of this book proved extremely successful, so much so that demand for strategic support with making best use of TAs evolved into a programme of training and consultancy. Our activities quickly adopted the acronym MITA (after the title of the book), and in 2014, we launched the MITA programme: a two-term school improvement programme based at the UCL Institute of Education in London. The experiences of the schools involved in the MITA programme have been key to updating this book, with many of the new case studies provided by the first cohorts of schools to complete the programme. We cover MITA in more detail in the following chapter.

Key features of the second edition

This book sets out guidance to help primary and secondary schools with the management and deployment of TAs, following the huge rise in support staff over recent years. It goes beyond previous guidance, and shows the need for a fundamental rethink of the current use and purpose of TAs, based on results from the largest study worldwide on TA impact: the DISS project.

This second edition builds on the processes and strategies contained in the first edition and reflects how our work with schools has refined and added to our understanding of what can be achieved when school leaders and teachers actively engage in the drive to improve the use of their TA workforce.

A key aim is to update and add new material to reflect the way in which things have moved on, even in the relatively short space of time since the first edition. The English education system has seen several areas of policy develop or change in ways that have implications for the deployment of TAs and provision for pupils with SEN, principally the introduction of a new SEN Code of Practice in September 2014. This new context is reflected in our new coverage.

This book is also essential reading for the growing number of school leaders and teachers who are interested in how to use findings from empirical research to inform their practice. One of the leaders in this field to have emerged since the publication of the first edition of this book is the Education Endowment Foundation (EEF), which is part of the Sutton Trust. The EEF's *Teaching and Learning Toolkit*[1] provides summaries of educational research to help practitioners make decisions about which interventions might be most successful in improving the attainment of underachieving pupils. Popular and informative though they are, the EEF's Toolkit and other similar online resources that 'rate' educational interventions, such as John Hattie's impressive *Visible Learning* project,[2] only go so far. Providing information about what works – and, indeed, what does not work – is one thing, but our experience of talking to school leaders has shown that what they *really* want to know is 'how do I make it work in my school'. Such resources – at least in relation to TAs – are thin on the ground.

As educational researchers, we understand the importance of having a conceptually and empirically strong framework for structuring decisions and action. School leaders share this understanding. With the drive to evidence-informed practice, those we speak to regularly comment on the value of having a process that has undergone extensive trialling and validation in schools, and is underpinned by the WPR model. Furthermore, we recognise how real world experiences are particularly effective ways of articulating common problems and creative solutions. This is why we have asked school leaders, teachers, special educational needs coordinators (SENCos) and TAs with whom we have collaborated to contribute their experiences of working through and applying the guidance in the first edition of this book. We have used these testimonies to develop the case studies you will find throughout this second edition.

We offer alternatives to common, but, we argue, mistaken methods of TA deployment, which are currently letting down lower-attaining pupils and those with SEN. We draw out recommendations for practice at the school and classroom level, and for policymakers nationally. We also anticipate that this book will be of international significance, at a time when more and more countries are introducing TAs to mainstream classrooms.

Finally, we have written this book in such a way as to be accessible to practitioners, with many examples and tools for use in professional development and in-service training.

Although there have been a number of practical guides on the use of TAs, this book is different because it is based on results from a programme of research and development which, for the first time, studied in detail the impact of TAs on pupils and teachers. We feel existing guides on this topic are outdated if they serve to maintain the status quo and fail to recognise and address the central problem identified by the DISS project.

Decision-making and action

The key driver for change is the school itself. When we examine the outcomes from our work with schools, the consistent and very clear message is this: if you are a headteacher or school leader, you need to fundamentally review how your school deploys TAs, what expectations you have of them, and, crucially, you need to then lead change.

School leaders (and many others in education) tend to see the truth in the findings from our research, and are willing to consider the implications for their schools. But too often we have found that action is delegated to middle leaders or SENCo, not necessarily connected to, or reporting directly to, the senior leadership team (SLT). This can mean change is piecemeal and sometimes puts the staff who have been delegated the responsibility for change in a difficult position, particularly if this requires taking decisions they do not have the power to take; for example, amending TAs' employment contracts or hours of work.

Often we find school leaders think that many of the issues relating to ineffective practice can be addressed almost exclusively through training at the level of the TA. We entirely agree with those who say TAs, like teachers, should have access to regular training to increase their knowledge and improve their practice. However, this alone is not sufficient to remediate the issues revealed by the DISS project.

It is the school and classroom structures within which TAs work that govern how effective they are, in terms of their impact on pupil outcomes. So deep rooted are the factors that determine TA effectiveness, it is unrealistic – not to mention unreasonable – to expect TAs to solve the problem of their use in schools through their efforts alone.

To avoid neutering the effects of the change you can potentially achieve from the process outlined in this book, change needs to be sanctioned and led from the top by the person who has the greatest decision-making powers: the headteacher.

Let us be clear: retaining the status quo, in terms of the current and widespread models of deploying TAs, is letting the most vulnerable children down. Current practices must be reevaluated in order to realise the huge potential of the many TAs working in schools.

The purpose of this book

This book has been designed to provide easy-to-use, evidence-informed materials and activities to improve the way TAs are deployed, prepared and interact with pupils.

A main aim of the EDTA project was to learn lessons, identify good practice and collect examples from schools in order to form the basis of a book of guidance. Our subsequent efforts to support schools to work through this guidance (via the MITA programme and through other consultancy activities) have helped us to modify, add to and in many ways strengthen the approach set out in the first edition of *Maximising the Impact of Teaching Assistants*. And as we anticipated, this work has generated further examples of good practice we are able to include in this new edition of the book. We offer solutions and ideas developed from these main sources of our work, as well as accessible summaries of key recommendations, examples of strategies successfully used in schools, and much-needed examples of effective practice in the form of short case studies.

This book also describes a school-based audit for self-evaluation: approaches, techniques and factors to consider when making an in-house assessment of TA deployment and preparation, and the provision for pupils with learning needs. The audit engages stakeholders in a dynamic process of review and performance improvement, identifying and building on existing good practice. The aim is that schools will be able to use this as a template for undertaking a survey of provision, as well as developing solutions and strategies for change based on the areas of good and not-so-good practice the audit reveals.

The aim of the audit process is to determine the extent to which the reality matches participants' perceptions, and to provoke discussion about how models of deployment and preparation could be modified and improved. We anticipate that once this process has started, schools will want to continue to evaluate their practice, and refine and develop new strategies in the light of new challenges. It is no coincidence that we have written this book to encourage reflective practice and to support continuing school improvement.

Our work shows there is no 'one size fits all' solution; as a school, you will need to arrive at local solutions to the general and specific problems we have identified through our research, and which may apply, to a greater or lesser extent, in your school. The overall standpoint of the book is to identify with the many school leaders and teachers who tell us that their schools would struggle to function without TAs, but to show why progress can only be made if we first recognise there is a problem with the current and widespread forms of TA deployment, and that alternative ways of utilising them need to be put in place and developed.

Our recommendations deliberately address the fact that schools – especially given the impact of cuts to public sector spending – are unlikely to receive any additional funding from government in the immediate future with which to implement workforce employment and deployment decisions. Our collaborative work with schools, acutely aware of the economic context within which they operate, recognises that developing and evaluating creative solutions to local problems is the most likely – and maybe the only realistic – way forward.

In the long run, it is also likely to be the most fruitful approach too, as it can lead to more profound and longer-term changes. Schools in the EDTA project, for example, decided to rethink and change existing ways of working in sustainable ways, rather than adopt additional practices that were likely to be short-lived. This book is an attempt to update and share the best of this work more widely.

Using this book

This book is primarily directed at headteachers and principals, in both primary and secondary schools, who make strategic decisions about the best ways to deploy TAs. Our other key constituency is teachers looking for techniques and strategies to improve the way they use TAs in the classroom. It will also be highly relevant to SENCos and inclusion managers who, depending on the size of the school they work in, may also have a teaching or senior leadership role. Here are some things to consider in order to support your use of the book.

Headteachers and school leaders

If you are a headteacher or principal and you have picked up this book with a view to reforming the way you use TAs in your school, we would first like to commend you for taking this matter seriously. No doubt you will already be aware this is no small task, but, as we have been emphasising in this opening section, it is a vital one if schools are to make the most of their TAs and have a positive, rather than detrimental, impact on learning. Therefore, before we go any further, it is worth sharing some of the experiences of the senior leaders who have taken part in the EDTA project and the MITA programme, who were once at the start of this journey.

A prerequisite of our work with schools is to engage staff who are already convinced of the need for change and are willing to undertake the developmental work on which wider and better practice can be built. In any work of this nature, it is worth identifying the people within an organisation who support the main vision and are willing to contribute actively to developing and testing new ideas as part of a change team. Having a small core of enthusiastic colleagues who are open to new ways of working with TAs – including TAs themselves – can be vital in not only testing out new ideas in the classroom, but also becoming advocates of change among your wider staff team, championing new ideas and getting other colleagues on board. If possible, and if relevant, aim to get representation from staff working in each Key Stage. The value of informal ways of gathering grassroots support for change cannot be overestimated.

Many of the schools we have worked with had regular SLT meetings dedicated to this work. One primary school formed a cross-school working party comprising the headteacher, SENCo, a senior teacher and a higher-level teaching assistant, who met termly to plan action and discuss progress. Schools participating in the MITA programme form a project team, which must minimally include the headteacher and SENCo.

If there is one thing that unites the schools we work with (other than their commitment to change), it is that they recognise that change takes time. In the EDTA project, we had three terms in which to plan, pilot, develop and evaluate the trials that schools introduced. In the MITA programme, we work with schools for two terms. In both cases, many school leaders acknowledge the task of rethinking and reforming the way TAs are used cannot be rushed or made to fit an artificial timeframe. Depending on your starting point, two or three terms is about right for conducting the groundwork for wider whole-school change.

In fact, a number of our MITA schools spent at least a term unpacking and getting a handle on the extent of the issues in their school. Unexpected though this was, they considered it time well spent, because it greatly informed their plans for the future. So, be sure to set aside regular time throughout the year to focus on your own project. This process of change should not be an 'add on' to other activities; it is a serious and systematic approach to whole-school improvement. And do not get despondent if you think progress is slow or things take longer than you hoped. For many schools, it is a long, but ultimately rewarding, journey.

The timing of introducing whole-school change is important too. It can be difficult to introduce changes midway through the school year. Many of the schools we have worked with spent a full school year planning, piloting, developing and evaluating new approaches and strategies, before a full implementation across the school at the start of the following year.

In the EDTA project, schools spent each term working on trials connected to one of the three main components of the WPR model: deployment, practice and preparedness. In the MITA programme, we encourage school leaders to work through the issues relating to deployment and practice first and foremost. Participants tell us this focus of attention on particular areas is helpful for isolating and dealing with particular issues. It is tempting to try to deal with a bit of everything all at once, but there is a process to be followed, and having the discipline to stick to it is helpful both in informing actions in the next step of the cycle, and making best use of your valuable time. This book follows the model used in the MITA programme. We recommend schools using this book adopt a similar approach, and, indeed, we have structured it in a way that prioritises the order in which action should be addressed (see chapter summaries below).

The spirit in which any process of change regarding the role of TAs is carried out in schools is invariably important to its success. Nobody likes to have change forced upon them, and schools have had enough of that from government to last a lifetime! Nor do we need to remind you that these are sensitive times. Spending cuts, threats to job security, the erosion of the influence of both local authorities and trade unions, all conspire to make these precarious times for those working in low-paid public sector jobs. So this is no time or environment in which to embark on a process that will alienate staff and have them fearing it could lead to redundancies.

We do not recommend this book be used as part of a staff rationalisation or competency process. It is important all school staff realise the process we advocate is a valuable exercise to inform whole-school improvement. The aim is to conduct a forensic examination of your current practice of TA usage and to identify the factors that enable and inhibit them from performing their role effectively. You should be aiming to build on what works well in your school and to move towards the kinds of practice that can unlock the enormous potential of your TA workforce.

Like the EDTA project before it, schools in the MITA programme are not required to examine their SEN provision per se. However, it is worth mentioning that the review of TA employment and deployment schools undertake inevitably raises questions about the ways in which they meet the needs of pupils with SEN. TAs have become deeply connected to the way schools organise provision for SEN, but as the DISS project and our Making a Statement study – which we will introduce in the next chapter – have shown, there are inherent risks in assuming TAs are either the *only* option or the *appropriate* option for meeting the needs of some of the most vulnerable pupils. Therefore, the audit and the process of change described in this book could be conducted as part of, or alongside, a wider review of school structures and processes connected to SEN provision.

Key recommendations for school leaders

- Form a cross-school change team to think through, plan and conduct trials in classrooms, and feed back their experiences.
- Have regular SLT and change team meetings to discuss the development of your whole-school approach and to evaluate the trials.
- Take a school year to conduct this preparatory work and be ready to start the next year with a full school-wide roll-out of new strategies.
- Be clear about your motivations for conducting this process. Reassure TAs it is not an assessment of how well they do their job, but an evaluation of how effectively the school supports them. Make it clear that this is about investing in them and recognising their role and contribution to whole-school improvement.

Teachers

The results from the DISS project made it clear that teachers are given very little guidance on working with TAs through either their initial teacher education (ITE) course or school induction (see below). Given that virtually every teacher works with a TA, this is a lamentable state of affairs. This book can be considered required reading for PGCE students and trainees taking school-based routes to qualified teacher status, such as *Schools Direct* and *Teach First*.

Teachers wanting to improve their classroom practice with regard to TA deployment and preparation do not have to be working in a school where SLT are planning an organisational review in order to make use of this book. Our advice and strategies for implementation at the class level, flagged in the salient chapters under sections headed 'Teacher-level decisions', can help teachers to add real value to their teaching.

If you are a recently qualified teacher or experienced practitioner, one task we would encourage you to do before applying new strategies and models of working is to reflect on your own practice. Some of the questions raised in Chapter 2 will help you to appraise your practice.

Trainers and other readers

One of the main findings from the DISS project was that despite TAs' high visibility in classrooms, 75 per cent of teachers reported having had no training to help them work with TAs as part of their pre-service training and on-going professional development. This points to a clear challenge for ITE. Teacher trainers and those involved in the delivery of continuous professional development can use material in this book to inform and support a range of training and courses. Indeed, we know a number of local authorities have used the book to organise training and conferences.

While this is not a book about SEN, it will appeal to educational psychologists (EPs). As we have written about elsewhere, in light of the reformed processes for meeting the needs of children and young people with SEN and disabilities, EPs have a pivotal role in supporting schools and parents in the transition to alternative practices, less reliant on near-constant TA support (Webster 2014a).

More widely, decision-makers at the regional and national level who are concerned with policy and practice regarding support staff in mainstream schools (both in the UK and in countries where TAs are prevalent in schools) will also find the book of great relevance to their work. At the local level, school governors will find much to inform their thinking.

It is worth mentioning too that while this is *not* a book written for TAs, there is now guidance available specifically designed to dovetail with the philosophy and practices we cover here.

The Teaching Assistant's Guide To Effective Interaction: How to Maximise Your Impact

Our response to need for practical guidance for TAs is *The Teaching Assistant's Guide To Effective Interaction: How to Maximise Your Impact*, by Paula Bosanquet, Julie Radford and Rob Webster (2016).

Consistent with the guidance in this book, *The Teaching Assistant's Guide...* clarifies the role of the TA as unique and distinct from, but complementary to, that of the teacher, and focuses on the pivotal and intrinsic role of TAs' talk and interaction with pupils in the learning process. With the emphasis on 'practical', the guidance contains training and development materials for TAs, which can be used as the basis for school-based inset and to support formal courses for TAs (e.g. NVQs and foundation degrees).

Underpinned by key theory and research, and written in an accessible way, it provides a clear framework to guide and support TAs to develop the skills required to scaffold learning effectively and to encourage and help pupils to become more independent. It contains lots of reflection activities and practical strategies and techniques for TAs to use and try.

We cross-reference to *The Teaching Assistant's Guide...* at relevant points throughout this book to give you a sense of how the two sets of guidance interlock. Indeed, taken together, the two books demonstrate how the path to transforming the way your school uses TAs, and to ensuring they make a distinct and valuable contribution to learning, requires taking action at different levels.

Contents of the book

Chapter 1: The case for change: why do schools need to rethink the role of TAs?

This chapter sets out the case for rethinking the current and widespread ways of using TAs. Here we use the Wider Pedagogical Role model to structure our explanation for the negative relationship between TA support and pupil progress found in the DISS project, and raise questions for readers to consider. We explain how the WPR model provided the structure for the EDTA project, and how it evolved into the process used in the MITA programme. We also look at the key findings and messages from our evaluations of these interventions.

Chapter 2: Conducting an audit of current practice

This book encourages school leaders to undertake work that will, in many cases, involve organisational change. Knowing the position from which you start is central to any project that takes you to a planned end point. This chapter, therefore, aims to raise your awareness of the need to review the way you currently deploy and prepare TAs and to use this as a starting point for change. We present a set of tools and guidance to help you evaluate key aspects of TAs' employment, deployment and preparation. We draw on the audit tools we use in the MITA programmme, which were in turn developed and informed by our empirical research, and through which we have confirmed their usefulness in helping schools initiate the process of review and change.

Chapter 3: Defining your vision

Defining a clear vision is the most important strategic step in achieving your goal of maximising the impact of TAs. This chapter introduces a framework for successful and lasting organisational change that underpins the process for rethinking and reforming your TA workforce. This chapter aims to challenge perceptions about the role of TAs, the ways they are deployed and the impact they have on pupil outcomes. In thinking more broadly about the potential of the TA role, this chapter invites school leaders to engage with a fundamental question about their role, purpose and contribution. We use the SEN Code of Practice (DfE/DoH, 2015) in use at the time of publication (autumn 2015) in order to demonstrate the incentives and opportunities there are for schools, and spaces within which they can think about alternative roles for TAs.

Chapter 4: The deployment of TAs

From Chapter 4, we set out the main body of this book using the structure of the WPR model. We begin with deployment, as this is the starting point from which all other decisions about TAs flow. Central to our case for more effective uses of TAs is an understanding of the effects on pupils of what is often called the 'Velcro' model of TA support. On the basis of findings from the DISS and Making a Statement projects, we present the 'default' practice of using TAs as informal support for lower-attaining pupils and those with SEN as the central issue facing senior leaders and teachers. Starting from broad decisions about the composition of the TA workforce, we work through alternative models of school and classroom organisation that challenge the common forms of TA deployment. We set out types of TA role and describe the contribution they can make to your school or classroom.

Chapter 5: The practice of TAs

The verbal interactions between TAs and pupils (what we refer to in the WPR model as 'practice') are at the heart of their role as effective supporters of learning. The nature and quality of TAs' interactions with pupils is the focus of Chapter 5. Although this aspect of TAs' work relates to, and is informed by, decisions and strategies at the classroom level, there are school-level decisions relating to strategic choices about questioning styles, monitoring and training that can be made to improve TAs' practice. This chapter talks to ways in which schools can work towards reducing the overall need for adult support by helping pupils to develop independent learning skills.

Chapter 6: The preparedness of TAs

This chapter deals with school-level issues such as: recruitment; induction; TAs' pedagogical and subject knowledge and skills; training; and creating preparation time. At the classroom level, the focus is on making the most of opportunities for teachers and TAs to communicate before and after lessons, and the nature and quality of information that flows between them.

Chapter 7: Conclusions

In this final short chapter we sum up with some general conclusions about the impact of carrying out the suggestions in this book in relation to rethinking the use of TAs, based on the experiences of schools with whom we have worked.

Notes

1 For more information, visit https://educationendowmentfoundation.org.uk/toolkit/toolkit-a-z/
2 For more information, visit http://visible-learning.org/hattie-ranking-influences-effect-sizes-learning-achievement

Chapter 1

The case for change

Why do schools need to rethink the role of TAs?

Background

The rise and rise of teaching assistants

The unprecedented increase in the number of teaching assistants (TAs) in UK schools represents one of the most profound changes to the educational landscape in the last 20 years. While the proportion of teachers in mainstream schools in England has remained relatively steady over the last decade or so (DfE 2015), the proportion of full-time equivalent TAs has more than trebled since 2000, to 220,100 (DfE 2015). At the time of writing (summer 2015), half of the workforce in publicly funded mainstream schools in England is comprised of people other than teachers, collectively known as support staff,[1] and TAs account for half of these people.[2] TAs therefore comprise a quarter of the overall school workforce.

In terms of phases, the official data show TAs make up 34 per cent of the nursery and primary school workforce, and 15 per cent of the secondary school workforce. Given their prevalence, it is perhaps not surprising to find that a significant proportion of the schools' budget in England is spent on TAs. The last available figures suggest around £4.4 billion, or 13 per cent of the £33.6 billion budget, is spent on employing TAs (DfE 2012).

There has been a similar increase in TA numbers elsewhere in the UK (The Scottish Government 2011; Statistics for Wales 2011). More widely, Giangreco et al.'s (2014) qualitative survey of international territories describes an increase in classroom support staff in schools in Australia, Italy, Sweden, Canada, Finland, Germany, Hong Kong, Iceland, Ireland, Malta, South Africa, as well as the USA. However, nowhere has the growth in TAs been more pronounced than in the UK.

Interestingly, on the basis of headcount data, there are currently more TAs in English nursery and primary schools than teachers: 251,600 vs. 242,500 (DfE 2015). In secondary schools, the headcount ratio is roughly one TA to every three teachers. The size of the workforce can be explained by the fact that 91 per cent of nursery/primary TAs and 69 per cent of secondary TAs work part-time. By comparison, 21 per cent of teachers work part-time (DfE 2015).

From parent-helper to part of the school workforce

The part-time nature of TAs' work is a legacy of how the role has emerged in the UK as a result of three particular practices and influences over the last 30 or so years. The earliest influence was greater parental involvement in classroom life, which led to a surge in parent-helpers. In the early 1980s, some schools (mainly infants and primaries) had as many as 50 parents a week providing assistance (Caudrey 1985). As well as providing a much-needed extra pair of hands for activities such as school trips and art and craft, parent-helpers also helped with reading. The essential need for children to develop this basic skill in order to access the curriculum perhaps explains why support from additional adults was directed towards struggling readers.

Alongside these developments was a second key factor driving the increase in support staff. Following the 1981 Education Act, schools experienced an increase in the number of pupils with SEN being taught in mainstream schools. The drive towards inclusion had a profound effect of changing not only the composition of the pupil population in mainstream schools, but also the composition of the school workforce. Volunteer arrangements were formalised into salaried positions as 'welfare assistants' and 'special needs assistants', and latterly 'learning support assistants' and 'teaching assistants'. Other general parent-helper roles evolved into 'classroom assistant' posts. There was, however, no consistency in how these 'assistant' job titles were applied across schools. Over time, people in these roles came to be known collectively as 'teaching assistants': a catchall title to refer to all classroom- or pupil-based support staff.

Thomas (1992) concludes the increase in the number of additional adults, and frequency with which they came to work alongside teachers in the classroom between the 1980s and 1990s, happened largely 'by stealth'. The number of 'non-teaching support staff' grew as schools welcomed the offer and availability of assistance from parents. It was perhaps somewhat inevitable that with so many willing volunteers, some of them were deployed to undertake (or drifted towards doing) instructional tasks, often with the pupils who showed the greatest need for extra help.

The third main driver of the increase in support staff came in the early part of the twenty-first century. In response to concerns over excessive teacher workload and the knock-on effect this was having on recruitment and retention, the government put in place a set of provisions to help schools manage teacher workload by freeing up time for planning and assessment, and removing their routine, time-consuming administrative tasks. The National Agreement (DfES 2003) enabled and encouraged schools to employ more TAs and other support staff, such as bursars, reprographics staff, site managers and examinations officers, to help deliver these provisions for teachers. A key expectation of this policy was that the use of support staff would drive up educational standards.

The increase in school support staff can be seen as part of a general rise in paraprofessionals across the public services, not just in the UK, but worldwide. Professional roles in education and other sectors (e.g. medicine, social work, law and the police) have been redefined, so others (e.g. nurses and paralegals) undertake some activities previously performed by established professionals (Bach et al. 2004).

The findings from the DISS study show the general effect of these initiatives over the last three decades has been that TAs now occupy a role in mainstream schools where they interact with pupils – principally those not making the expected levels of progress and those with learning and behavioural difficulties. On the face of it, this may look like a good arrangement, because TAs provide more opportunities for one-to-one and small group work, both in and out of the classroom. However, as we have seen, it has also led to negative consequences for pupils at the receiving end of that support.

While the widening use of 'non-teachers' is the result of pragmatic and well-meaning responses to particular needs at the school level, the evolution of the TA role has profoundly changed the dynamics of classroom interaction (see Webster 2015). Furthermore, this has, to a large extent, occurred with little debate or public discussion, or recourse to the evidence of the impact of TA support on pupils' learning.

Research on the impact of TA support

While there is evidence that TAs have a positive impact on teachers' workload and stress levels (Blatchford et al. 2012b), until the DISS project, there was next to no empirical research on the impact of TAs on pupils over sustained periods (e.g. a school year) and under everyday classroom conditions. Much of the evidence that does exist concerns mostly small-scale studies of TA-led curriculum interventions. There are some important points to make about the body of research on TAs, which is helpful for contextualising the case made and guidance presented in this book.

When it comes to the research on the direct impact of TAs on learning outcomes, we can separate most of it into two broad categories: (i) studies measuring the effects of curriculum interventions and 'catch-up' programmes delivered by TAs; and (ii) studies focusing on the impact from other forms of TA deployment. The first group tends to concern studies involving specific subjects – typically numeracy and aspects of literacy (reading, spelling, writing and phonics) – and pupils in certain year groups. In many cases, these intervention programmes are very often delivered outside the classroom. The second group of studies concerns research on how TAs are used inside the classroom in everyday conditions.

Research on TA-led interventions

Simply put, there is good evidence pupils make progress in literacy and numeracy as a result of structured curriculum interventions delivered by TAs – but *only* when TAs have been properly trained to deliver those programmes (see Alborz et al. 2009).

Often the positive results from research on TA-led interventions are frequently offered up as conclusive proof of TA impact (Ward 2014), but the overall evidence base is surprisingly thin. The majority of this research comes from international studies conducted on a small-scale, typically involving small samples of 30 to 200 pupils (Sharples et al. 2015). These limitations have implications for the generalisability of the results: how confident can we be that a particular intervention will produce positive outcomes for every pupil in every setting, every time it is used?

The research investigating TAs delivering interventions may be small, but it is growing. Results from randomised control trials (RCT) funded by the Education Endowment Foundation in the UK are among some of the most recent research in this area, and emerging findings from evaluations are consistent with the international picture. RCTs allow researchers to compare results from a group of pupils who received support from TAs trained in an intervention programme with results from control groups who did not receive the programme (but may at a later date) or who received an alternative form of support. Results from well-designed RCTs do not imply certainty of success when applied to your own setting, but they can improve our level of confidence when it comes to making good decisions about using a particular intervention and the conditions under which it works best.

It is easy to get seduced by the results of impact assessments. Evaluations of intervention programmes appearing to show, for example, 12 months of progress in reading in just three months of delivery are bound to appeal to school leaders. But there are important caveats to add regarding how the study or RCT was designed, and the way the intervention was delivered, which can affect the outcomes. These caveats are worth discussing in brief, as they can help us be more mindful when thinking about the implications of results from such studies, as well as improve decision-making about which programmes to buy and use.

Firstly, impacts on pupil progress tend to only be measured *in relation to* the intervention programme itself. Most 'off the shelf' intervention packages come with a tool to take baseline and progress measures, but these only relate to the content and coverage of the programme. Furthermore, any effects cannot be extrapolated with 100 per cent reliability due to the restricted nature of the conditions under measurement. Results from a specific programme delivered to pupils in a specific year group (possibly in a specific school in a specific area) are unable to tell us much about how effective it is outside of these parameters. In other words, the intervention might be successful for some pupils, but not others.

Secondly, only a few studies of curriculum interventions, including some RCTs, separate the effects of TA support from the intervention itself. So we cannot always be sure how much pupil progress is down to the programme and how much to TA support. Thirdly, many of these studies fail to ask whether the impact would have been greater if the programme had been delivered by a teacher, rather than a TA. Indeed, there are studies that show experienced and specifically trained teachers get better results than TAs when delivering the same programme (Higgins et al. 2013; Slavin et al. 2009).

Finally, there is the effect of what is called 'fidelity to the programme'. This describes how faithful the delivery of the programme is to the protocols and instructions that come with it. Interventions will have been tested and refined before being made available to schools; this is especially the case for commercial programmes. Careful in-house testing and evaluations by independent assessors will have been conducted on the basis that the intervention has been delivered as its creators intended. For example, an intervention might state it should be delivered to groups of three pupils, three times a week, for 20 minutes. So if schools want to achieve similar results to those reported in tests and evaluations, it is essential they deliver the programme in *exactly* the same way, and do not tinker with these essential factors; for example, delivering it to groups of six pupils, twice a week, for 40 minutes. If changes are made to any part of the programme, the programme itself changes, and the chances of success diminish.

While these factors can water down the effects of a programme, generally speaking, the impact of using properly trained TAs to deliver curriculum interventions has a positive effect on learning outcomes. There are some additional points the research on interventions raises about the use of such programmes, which we address in Chapter 4.

It is important to bear in mind it can take several weeks, months or terms to complete the delivery of an intervention; it varies. It is worth noting research has yet to shed light on how immediate improvements via interventions translate into long-term learning and performance on national tests. This is particularly relevant given that pupils' learning in interventions is not regularly connected to the wider curriculum and learning in the classroom, as we shall see. What is more, studies of interventions are restricted in being able to tell us anything about the effect of TA support over a school year. In order to find this out, we have to look at the other body of research on impact.

Research on TAs in everyday classrooms

Although evidence for the effects of TA-led interventions on pupil learning is broadly positive, data from the large-scale DISS project showed delivering interventions – work which tends to be done outside the classroom, remember – accounted for only around 40 minutes of a TA's day. This is echoed in findings from Farrell et al. (2010).

There are only a few studies that have systematically measured the direct impact of TA support on pupil attainment under normal classroom conditions, that is, separate from any specific impact from interventions. Findings from large-scale systematic analyses investigating the effects of TAs on learning outcomes challenge the assumption there are unqualified benefits from TA support. Experimental studies are rare, but the Tennessee Student-Teacher Achievement Ratio (STAR) project in the USA found no differences in the outcomes for pupils in classes with TAs present (Finn et al. 2000; Gerber et al. 2001). Longitudinal research from the UK Class Size and Pupil-Adult Ratios project produced similar results (Blatchford et al. 2004).

Secondary analyses of school expenditure have suggested the expenditure on TAs is positively correlated with improved academic outcomes (Brown and Harris 2010; Nicoletti and Rabe 2015). However, these analyses of TA impact do not adequately rule out the possibility that other school factors might explain the correlations found, and the conclusions drawn are often not supported by the evidence collected; in particular, they do not include data on *what actually happens* in classrooms.

As we saw in the Introduction, the DISS project is the largest and most authoritative study on the impact of TA support on learning outcomes and it showed consistent negative relationships between the amount of TA support pupils received and their academic progress over a school year in English, mathematics, and science – even after controlling for potentially confounding factors, such as prior attainment and SEN.

There was evidence too that the effect was more marked for pupils with the highest levels of SEN (Webster et al. 2010), but it was still generally evident for pupils without SEN who received TA support.

For now, the UK evidence base on the effects of TA support over a school year is currently limited to the DISS project. Nonetheless, based on what we do know, we might reasonably conclude there are questions over whether progress made in TA-led interventions away from the class translates into overall end-of-year attainment.

Accounting for the negative relationship between TA support and pupil progress

The extensive research conducted as part of the DISS project allows us to provide a compelling explanation for the negative relationship between TA support and pupil progress. To begin with, we might reasonably assume pupils who were given the most TA support in the first place would have been those most likely to make less progress in any case. However, such explanations, in terms of pre-existing characteristics of pupils, are unlikely because the factors that typically affect progress (and the allocation of TA support), such as SEN status, prior attainment and measures of deprivation, were controlled for in the statistical analyses. To be of any consequence, any potential factor causing or influencing this relationship would need to be systemic across *all* year groups and *all* subjects, and related to *both* pupil attainment *and* the allocation of TA support.

Another possible explanation for the negative relationship is it may be due to the different levels of TAs' qualifications relative to teachers. We note, however, that research has not found that teachers' or TAs' levels of qualification are related to their effectiveness (Blatchford et al. 2004; Muijs and Reynolds 2001; Wiliam 2010). There is a more extensive discussion of alternative explanations in Blatchford et al. (2012b).

So, if pupil factors and TA qualifications do not appear to be explaining the negative relationship between TA support and pupil progress, what is?

We argue it is the decisions made by headteachers and teachers relating to TAs' employment and deployment, which offer the most fruitful answers to this question.

We developed the Wider Pedagogical Role (WPR) model to explain the DISS project results and also to provide the basis for the guidance and recommendations set out in this book. The WPR model also provides the structural and theoretical underpinning for decision-making and action in what we call the 'MITA process' (more of which later). The basic components of the WPR model are shown in Figure 1.1 (taken from Blatchford et al. 2012b).

We now present the key findings from the DISS project thematically, using the three main components of the WPR model: *deployment, practice* and *preparedness*.[3] For each component, we raise questions and points of discussion for you to think about in relation to the situation in your school or classroom.

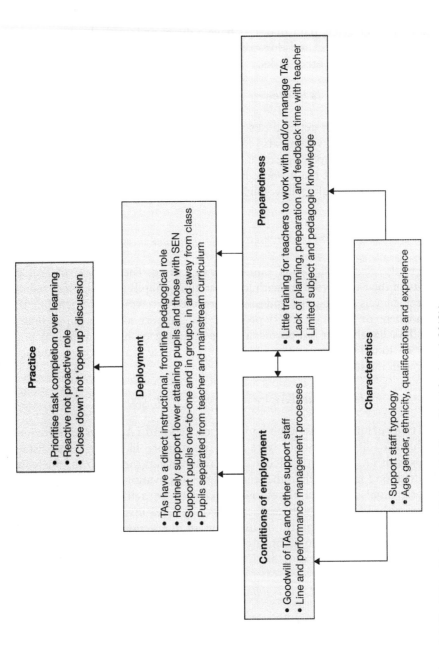

Practice
- Prioritise task completion over learning
- Reactive not proactive role
- 'Close down' not 'open up' discussion

Deployment
- TAs have a direct instructional, frontline pedagogical role
- Routinely support lower attaining pupils and those with SEN
- Support pupils one-to-one and in groups, in and away from class
- Pupils separated from teacher and mainstream curriculum

Preparedness
- Little training for teachers to work with and/or manage TAs
- Lack of planning, preparation and feedback time with teacher
- Limited subject and pedagogic knowledge

Conditions of employment
- Goodwill of TAs and other support staff
- Line and performance management processes

Characteristics
- Support staff typology
- Age, gender, ethnicity, qualifications and experience

Figure 1.1 The Wider Pedagogical Role model (from Blatchford et al. 2012b)

Deployment

Deployment concerns how TAs are used across the school and in classrooms, and the decision-making behind this. The findings on deployment led us to some stark conclusions about the role of TAs. It is clear from work pattern diaries, systematic observations and interview data that TAs have a direct pedagogical role, supporting and interacting with pupils, and this exceeds time spent supporting the teacher and curriculum, or performing other tasks.

Is this the case in your school?

What is more, results from detailed observations showed teachers tended to interact with pupils in whole-class contexts and infrequently worked with them on an individual basis or in groups. Instead, it is TAs who spend more time working with (mostly small) groups and one-to-one, both in and away from the classroom. It is these contexts that generally allow higher quality interaction between adults and pupils to take place.

Does this general finding match what happens in your school?

Results were also clear about *which* pupils TAs supported. The majority of TAs spent the majority of their time working with lower-attaining pupils (that is, those failing to make expected levels of progress) and pupils identified as having SEN (including those with a Statement of SEN). Teachers provided less support to these pupils than did TAs, and TAs hardly ever supported average-attaining or higher-attaining pupils. Crucially, we found TA interaction with pupils increased, and teacher interaction decreased, with the severity of pupils' SEN.[4]

Is this how TAs are deployed in your school?

The broad types of interactions pupils had with teachers and TAs, in terms of frequency and length, also differed. Pupils were nine times more likely to have sustained interactions with TAs than with teachers. 'Sustained' means the pupil was the focus of the TA's attention for longer than the length of the observation interval (ten seconds). Furthermore, pupils were six times more likely to be actively involved in their interactions with TAs than with teachers. Here, 'active' involvement is defined in terms of beginning, responding to or sustaining an interaction with an adult during the observation interval. In contrast, for the vast majority of their interactions with teachers, pupils were one of a crowd.

Do you know if this is what happens in your classrooms?

This kind of one-to-one support from TAs might seem pedagogically valuable, but there are serious and unintended consequences. A main consequence is that supported pupils become separated from the teacher, missing out on everyday teacher-to-pupil interactions. Where pupils are withdrawn from lessons to work with TAs outside the classroom (say, to do an intervention), they spend less time in mainstream curriculum coverage. What is more, many TAs have been given, or have absorbed, the responsibility for planning out of class coverage. This is particularly the case for pupils with SEN: TAs have, in effect, become the primary educators of some of the most disadvantaged and vulnerable pupils in schools, and the impact of TA support on their academic progress is much worse compared to 'non-supported' pupils. A key conclusion from the findings on TA deployment was that TA support is *alternative* to teacher input – not, as is often suggested, 'additional' to it.

Are you surprised by these results?

THE MAKING A STATEMENT STUDY

In light of these particular results on the deployment of TAs from the DISS project, it is useful to introduce a brief summary of findings from a more recent observational study on the educational experiences of pupils with a Statement of SEN, conducted by two of the authors (Rob Webster and Peter Blatchford). The Making a Statement (MAST) study tracked 48 pupils in Year 5 in mainstream primary schools with Statements for moderate learning difficulties or behavioural, emotional and social difficulties.[5]

The study involved making minute-by-minute observations on what pupils were experiencing: where they were (e.g. in or out of the class); what they were doing (e.g. working alone, with a group, or as part of the class); and which adults were involved. For comparison, data were also collected on 151 average-attaining, non-SEN pupils.

The results show the educational experience of pupils with Statements is characterised by a high degree of separation (Webster and Blatchford 2013). Compared to the average-attaining pupils, they spent the equivalent of over a day a week away from their classroom. As a result of a high-level of support from TAs – the so-called 'Velcro' effect – we found that compared to the average-attainers, those with Statements spent less time in whole-class teaching with teachers, and were more than three times more likely to interact with TAs than with teachers. Statemented pupils had about half as many opportunities to interact with their peers as the average-attaining pupils.

One in every five interactions a Statemented pupil had was with a TA. For the other pupils, interactions with a TA made up a very small part of their classroom experience: one in every 50 interactions they had was with a TA.

We will discuss the implications of these and other findings from the MAST study later on.

What do you know about the day-to-day experiences of pupils with Statements or Education, Health and Care Plans in your school?

Practice

The DISS project findings on 'practice' (i.e. interactions between TAs and pupils) make it clear that pupils' one-to-one interactions with TAs are not only longer, more sustained and more interactive compared with their interactions with teachers, but these interactions differ in *quality*. We found four overarching characteristics of TAs' talk to pupils:

1   Interactions between TAs and pupils were not clearly linked to the learning aims of the task. TAs' talk was frequently more concerned with *task completion* than with ensuring any learning and understanding had taken place.
2   TAs' interactions with pupils could be broadly characterised as *reactive*, because – unlike teachers, who guided lessons with planned learning aims in mind – TAs had to routinely respond to the needs of the pupils and the lesson in the moment.
3   TAs did more *prompting*, and when they did, it could sometimes tip over into spoon-feeding, where TAs would take on too much responsibility for doing the task for the pupil.
4   Teachers generally '*open up*' pupil talk, whereas the TAs '*close down*' the talk, both linguistically and cognitively. One expression of this was TAs' tendency to use a high proportion of closed questions to open questions, compared with teachers, who used more open questions.

Have you ever listened carefully to a TA working with a pupil?

There was also evidence TAs' explanations were, on occasions, inaccurate or misleading. On the basis of this evidence, it is hard to avoid the view that TAs tend not to know how to make the best use of the extended, more frequent interactions they have with pupils. It is important to put these findings on practice into context. To do this, we need to consider how effectively TAs are prepared for the roles they undertake.

Preparedness

Preparedness describes two aspects critical to TAs' work and effectiveness:

*   the training and professional development TAs and teachers receive, including how teachers manage and organise the work of TAs
*   day-to-day preparation: the time for, and quality of, planning and feedback between teachers and TAs.

TEACHER AND TA TRAINING

Given the growth of TAs and their high visibility in classrooms, it might be expected that training to help teachers work with TAs would form part of pre-service and/or inset training. However, the DISS project surveys of teachers showed 75 per cent of them reported having had no such training.

What kind of preparation, if any, have your teachers had to work with TAs?

The surveys also revealed over half of teachers and SENCos line managed one or more TAs. Yet, again, two-thirds of these line managers had not received any training for this role. Teachers who had received training in relation to working with and/or line managing TAs reported mixed views. For both types of training, the majority of respondents said it lasted only one day or less, and only half rated the training as useful.

How have your teachers been prepared for this part of their role?

DAY-TO-DAY PREPARATION

The second aspect of preparedness concerns how TAs are prepared for the roles they take on in the classroom, which as we have seen, are often pedagogical or instructional in nature. One of the DISS project's key findings was 75 per cent of teachers reported having no allocated planning or feedback time with the TAs they worked with. This was most marked for secondary schools, within which 95 per cent of teachers claimed they had no such time. Communication between teachers and TAs was largely *ad hoc*; conversations took place during lesson changeovers, before and after school, and during break and lunch times, and so, for the most part, relied on the goodwill of TAs.

How do the arrangements for TA preparation and feedback in your school compare with this situation?

In interviews, many TAs reported feeling under-prepared for the tasks they were given. With little or no time to talk with teachers before lessons, TAs described how, in many cases, they 'went into lessons blind'. They had to 'tune in' to the teacher's delivery in order to pick up vital subject and pedagogical knowledge, and information and instructions relating to the tasks they supported pupils with. Exactly the same situation was found in the MAST study (Webster and Blatchford 2014).

Have you ever tried to find out how the TAs in your school feel about the time for and quality of lesson preparation and feedback to teachers?

Summary

We can now see the DISS project findings suggest three main explanations for the troubling and unexpected findings on the impact of TA support on pupil learning. These explanations were bolstered with evidence from the MAST study:

1   Despite much debate about the appropriate role of TAs, it is clear they have a predominantly pedagogical role, directly interacting with pupils – principally those with learning needs. As a consequence, such pupils become separated from the teacher and the curriculum. The MAST study was able to show the extent of this separation for pupils with the highest level of SEN.
2   TAs' interactions with pupils (their practice) are less academically demanding, with the emphasis on completing tasks, rather than ensuring any learning or understanding takes place. The additional evidence from the MAST study makes it hard to avoid the conclusion pupils with SEN have a lower quality learning diet, compared to their peers.
3   The opportunity for and quality of teachers' and TAs' preparedness is severely limited. While both require different forms of preparation, their performance in

the classroom is hampered by a lack of knowing how to work together, the amount of time available to discuss pupils and tasks, and for TAs, a clear understanding of what to do in lessons.

We developed the Wider Pedagogical Role model to explain the troubling results on pupils' academic progress found through the DISS project. The WPR model sets TA effectiveness (in terms of pupil outcomes) within a wider context, which takes account of the factors that govern their employment and deployment, and over which they have little or no control. The model (see Figure 1.1) shows the key findings from the DISS project (described above) and how the components of TAs' work relate to one another.

The Effective Deployment of Teaching Assistants project

This book is largely based on work conducted as part of the Effective Deployment of Teaching Assistants (EDTA) project. This one-year action research project gave us the opportunity to support the development of more effective models of TA usage in primary and secondary schools. The idea for the EDTA project emerged out of conversations with educationalists and practitioners confirming our belief there was a pressing need for clear, well-informed guidance on effective ways of deploying and preparing TAs.

The aims of the EDTA project were:

1   To work with headteachers, teachers and TAs in order to develop effective strategies for TA deployment in primary and secondary schools.
2   To evaluate the strategies and models of practice, and the processes by which they were introduced and developed, describing what worked well in the local implementation process.

The intervention

Two pairs of teacher-TA teams were recruited from ten schools (six primary and four secondary) in two local authorities (LAs) in England. The intervention ran over the 2010–11 school year. In September 2010, we held meetings for school leaders, SENCos and participating teachers in each LA, at which we presented the DISS project findings, plus the rationale and aims of the EDTA project. We decided not to include TAs in these meetings, as our intention was to cut through to those with decision-making responsibilities and initiate discussion and debate. We did, however, hold meetings for participating TAs to impart the research information.

A key feature of the EDTA project was the way we used the three core components of the WPR model (deployment, practice and preparedness) as focal points for work each term. At termly meetings, we encouraged participants to develop trials relating to a particular component, which would address one or more pertinent issues arising from the DISS project. Trials were conducted over the term, and halfway through, a member of the research team visited the school to observe and discuss progress with each teacher-TA pair.

The evaluation

We adopted a within-school comparative approach, evaluating practice before and after the introduction of the trials. The evaluation compared new models developed through trials, with existing models of TA deployment and how teachers and TAs worked together. The main question addressed was whether involvement in the intervention led to more effective deployment, practice and preparation of TAs.

We collected evaluation data using surveys, semi-structured interviews and quantitative structured lesson observations, all of which were conducted at the start and end of the intervention. In addition to the formal evaluation, researchers asked teacher-TA pairs to evaluate the success of their trials and identify any facilitative or inhibiting factors to successful implementation, thereby helping us to understand the wider contexts in which change does or does not happen in schools. Our findings were shared with participants at a final meeting.

Key findings

We summarise the main project findings at the end of Chapters 4, 5 and 6, in order to show how the guidance collated in this book changed things in schools and classrooms. We present a summary of overall findings from the EDTA project in Chapter 7 and in Webster et al. (2013). The full final report (Blatchford et al. 2012a) is available from our website: www.maximisingtas.co.uk.

However, as we build the case for change, it is worth sharing some of the key findings here. As a result of participating in the intervention:

- Teachers were more aware of their responsibilities towards lower-attaining pupils and those with SEN, and worked more often with these pupils.
- There were improvements in the quality of TAs' interactions with pupils.
- Schools created teacher–TA liaison time.
- Teachers provided TAs with clearer and more detailed lesson plans.
- TAs' esteem, value and confidence improved from having a more clearly defined role.

Perhaps the key message from the EDTA project for school leaders and teachers is this: changing the way you deploy and prepare TAs is not only possible, but has significant benefits for *all* school staff and *all* pupils.

The Maximising the Impact of Teaching Assistants (MITA) programme

The broad principles and processes deployed in the EDTA project, codified in this book, form the basis of the MITA school improvement programme we run at the UCL Institute of Education (IOE), London.

The MITA programme supports school leaders through a process of rethinking and reforming how they use TAs. The headteacher/principal and the SENCo from each school gather together at the IOE (other members of SLT also attend, depending on the school) over two terms to work through the critical strategic and organisational implications of getting best value from TAs, and to ensure they make a meaningful contribution to teaching and learning. For more on the programme, visit our website: www.maximisingtas.co.uk.

As in the EDTA project, the first session is used to present the evidence base on TA use and impact, along with some additional scene-setting, in terms of how the coverage of the programme sits within the contemporary political and educational contexts. This, as we shall see, is important, as it demonstrates how the need to rethink and reform the role of TAs prevails, and how wider educational initiatives and policies allow and create space for school leaders to address this vital issue. The MITA programme is responsive, and has grown and adapted to take account of developments and policies affecting schools' decision-making regarding TAs; a good example is the new SEN Code of Practice.

Early on in the 'MITA process', schools are encouraged to conduct a thorough audit of the current situation in their school. We discuss how to audit practice in Chapter 2, along with various tools to use.

Over the two terms of the programme, schools are supported by our team of experienced practitioners, advisors, trainers and consultants (many of whom also have a research background) to develop a clear vision on what they want the role of TAs to be in their school. *Defining a clear vision is the most important strategic step in achieving your goal of maximising the impact of TAs.* We look at this part of the process in depth in Chapter 3.

In further sessions at the IOE, we explore the management of change in schools, school and classroom practices to improve TA deployment and preparedness, and their interaction with pupils. This provides participants with frameworks and ideas for additional school-based training. Over the two terms, schools develop and test strategies, coming together at the group sessions to share their ideas and establish links and collaborations. The findings from our evaluation of the MITA programme are highlighted at relevant points throughout the book, with a summary of the main points in Chapter 7.

The second edition of this book enables us to update the guidance in the first edition with new ideas and strategies based on the experiences of schools that have worked through it. We have drawn not only on the work achieved by schools participating in the MITA programme at the IOE, but also from schools in Essex, where the local authority runs a successful parallel version of MITA. We have also included the experiences and ideas of school leaders from across the UK we have met or who have emailed us; some having achieved great things just by working through this book, with little external support. We have used all these 'real world' examples to create the case studies you will see throughout this book.

Following the MITA process

This book follows what we call 'the MITA process': from how to conduct an audit (Chapter 2), to setting a vision for your TA workforce (Chapter 3), then on to how to address issues relating to the three main components of the WPR model, just as schools in the EDTA project did (Chapters 4, 5 and 6).

A key aim for this book is to encourage you to develop a clear vision for the TA workforce in your school. We recommend you start with the end in mind. Effective leadership is all about defining a blueprint, gaining consensus around change and ensuring everyone within the school is working in ways consistent with the vision. Our experience has shown that these are 'active ingredients' in producing practices that stick (Webster 2014b). Schools that take the vision-defining step seriously tend to create favourable conditions for change; that is, staff get onside early. *A key theme of this book is this: changing the way you use TAs in your school is necessarily a leadership issue.*

Rethinking policy and practice on TAs: the political and educational context

The EDTA project and MITA have extended the messages arising out of the DISS project and have given renewed impetus to policy changes and other educational initiatives. Our work on TAs informed the Lamb Inquiry on parental confidence in the SEN system and the 2014 SEN Code of Practice. Our research is also frequently mentioned in relation to how schools spend Pupil Premium funding. We have also worked with the Education Endowment Foundation to help improve school leaders' and teachers' understanding and use of empirical evidence to inform decision-making about improving outcomes for disadvantaged children and young people (Sharples et al. 2015).

Getting issues relating to TA employment and deployment on the policy map has taken time. As the second edition of this book went to press, we were awaiting the outcome of the review of TA standards, commissioned by the government in October 2014.

While such efforts recognise the contribution of TAs to schools – and may go some way to formalising their role as paraprofessionals – we are concerned they do not offer any challenge to the status quo in terms of how TAs are deployed, especially in relation to pupils with SEN. We are deeply concerned that the failure to engage fully with the fundamental questions raised by the DISS project will reinforce current models of practice, which continue to let down disadvantaged children. In the current political climate, change seems ever more likely to be devolved to individual schools, and so it is our belief that our work will be of great assistance to school leaders looking for a framework for change.

There is a wider educational consideration here. We know lower-attaining pupils and those with SEN tend to be supported by TAs, rather than teachers. As Giangreco and colleagues (2005; Giangreco 2010) have argued, an implicit form of discrimination has developed: the most vulnerable and disadvantaged pupils receive less educational input from teachers than other pupils. If there are grounds for saying pupils with SEN are not appropriately served by this arrangement, there are also grounds for saying lower-attaining pupils are equally poorly served.

Therefore, if we are serious about addressing the well-known 'tail' in educational (under) achievement, then we should take very seriously the experiences of lower-attaining pupils and those with SEN, and the way in which current models of deploying TAs may not be helping their educational progress as much as we may have thought. *It should be of great concern to us that these pupils are negatively affected by the very intervention designed to help them.*

An extreme take on the DISS project findings on pupil progress, as described in our book, *Reassessing the Impact of Teaching Assistants* (Blatchford et al. 2012b), could be to drastically cut the number of TAs. In summer 2013, this idea was suggested by the Reform think-tank in a report on how to reduce the cost of running the UK education system (Thorpe et al. 2013). This prompted some alarming front-page headlines, including 'Classroom assistants face axe' in *The Sunday Times* (Woolf and Griffiths 2013). Thankfully, no action on this recommendation was taken in the UK, but in 2014, state legislators in North Carolina, USA used a one-sided interpretation of the DISS project findings to cut thousands of TA jobs in second and third grade classes (six- to eight-year-olds) (Curliss 2014).

Our view is that schools have much to gain from TAs, and few, if any, would wish to lose them. We agree with the sentiment we hear time and again from headteachers who tell us that without TAs, their school would not function successfully. Reframing the role and purpose of TAs is therefore essential to not only avoid accusations of wasteful expenditure and a negative impact on pupils, but, moreover, to make a strong case for giving TAs their own identity and value, demonstrable through a measurable impact on pupils.

To restate a central message from the DISS project: the reasons why support from TAs has a negative effect on pupil progress is not the fault of individual TAs; it is due to the systemic decisions made at the school level and the classroom level, by school leaders and teachers – not TAs – about how TAs are deployed and prepared.

The unintentional drift towards the situations revealed by the DISS project – in particular, how TAs have become the primary educators of lower-attaining pupils and those with SEN – arguably owes much to a lack of direction from government. In this sense, there are key messages for policymakers beyond the school level. For example, initial teacher education providers need to do more to prepare new teachers to be managers of TAs within their classrooms. This also extends to teachers' confidence and ability to work with pupils with SEN, and, more broadly, understanding the difference between 'underachievement' and 'having SEN', and how this affects provision planning.

We believe it is important to establish clear roles for teachers and TAs, and to produce the systems to support and maintain the demarcation, so each role – though different and complementary – is valued and respected on its own terms. It is also our strong belief that it is schools that are best placed to undertake this work. When they do, as the overarching message from the EDTA project and the MITA programme shows, change *is* possible. As it happens, the trend in government thinking is that schools themselves – not Whitehall – are best placed to run their own affairs. And as we will see in Chapter 3, the autonomy schools have is favourable to implementing the MITA process.

However, specific guidance from government and central agencies on how to go about making best use of TAs is thin on the ground. To be successful, schools need clear, well-informed guidance. We feel our book fills this vital gap.

The overall challenge facing school leaders, which we will explore, is how to define the role, purpose and contribution of TAs and show how it adds value to pupils' educational and social development in a distinctive way. We suggest the strategy of first envisaging the classroom as it would be with the teacher, but without the TA. First, decisions need to be taken about how the teacher would need to organise things in order to provide the best educational experience for *all* pupils in the class. Following this, the TA could then be reintroduced (so to speak) in such a way that they then provide a means by which the teacher can ensure this provision. The aim as we see it is to identify ways in which the TA *adds value* to what the teacher provides, rather than replacing the teacher.

A note on MITA and provision for pupils with SEN

It is worth saying from the outset that the work we outline in this book should *not* be seen as a proxy for rethinking how your school meets the needs of pupils with SEN. We say this because in some schools, TAs and support for children and young people with SEN have become so enmeshed that a co-dependency has developed. This was evident in findings from the MAST study. In such instances, the use of TAs tends to be restricted to supporting pupils with SEN, so schools fail to consider: (i) other forms of support for these pupils (e.g. more teacher input); and (ii) alternative roles for TAs.

Before we move on to the next chapter, school leaders must be aware that the aim of maximising the impact of TAs is not limited to the type of work TAs can do to support pupils with SEN. Our aim is broader: we see TAs as having a potentially transformative effect by taking on the type of roles that can benefit *all* pupils.

Finally, while the coverage of this book alights on the need for schools to improve SEN provision, we do not provide detail on, for example, the aspects of high quality teaching such pupils need and deserve.

Notes

1 All full-time equivalent teachers and support staff in publicly funded schools, including all local authority maintained schools, academies and city technology colleges.
2 The definition of 'teaching assistant' referred to here, and used in this book, includes all classroom-based and pupil-based support staff, known variously as teaching assistants, learning support assistants and classroom assistants. This definition also extends to staff in similar roles, including: higher-level teaching assistants; nursery nurses; nursery assistants; early years practitioners; literacy and numeracy support staff; learning mentors; special needs assistants; minority ethnic pupils support staff; plus any other non-teaching staff regularly employed to support teachers.
3 A more in-depth presentation and analysis of the DISS project findings, thematically arranged to cover all components of the WPR model, can be found in our book: *Reassessing the Impact of Teaching Assistants* (Blatchford et al. 2012b).
4 At the time of the DISS project, there were three levels denoting SEN severity, which were, in order of escalation: School Action, School Action Plus and Statement of SEN. With the introduction of the new SEN Code of Practice in 2014, the two School Action categories were collapsed into a new single category called 'SEN Support'.
5 Not only are these categories of SEN now no longer widely used, the introduction of the new SEN Code of Practice in 2014 replaced Statements with Education, Health and Care Plans.

Chapter 2

Conducting an audit of current practice

Introduction

This chapter covers the rationale for, and process of, a whole-school audit of TA usage. While it applies mainly to school leaders, there are practical ideas that can be easily adapted by individual teachers to appraise and develop how they use TAs in their own classrooms.

Why conduct an audit?

Our extensive research into the deployment and impact of TAs has shown the inadvertent effects of TA support are inextricably linked to the decisions made about TAs' deployment and preparation. These decisions, made with the best intentions, do not lie within the control of TAs, but instead with school leaders and teachers.

Yet, as the DISS project findings revealed, the impressions school leaders and teachers had about the effectiveness of TAs were at variance with the objective measures of TA impact. In short, what school leaders and teachers *believed* to be effective ways of using TAs were in fact – pedagogically speaking – doing more harm than good.

For this reason in particular, it is important that before any changes are made, you obtain as full a picture as possible of how TAs are currently deployed and prepared in your school, and of the nature and quality of their interactions with pupils, through an audit of teaching and TA staff. It is likely too that given the link between TA deployment and processes of inclusion for pupils with SEN, an audit of TA usage will provide an additional commentary on how effectively the school and teachers meet the needs of vulnerable pupils.

The results of a TA audit will provide you with a starting point in terms of identifying the areas requiring change and the extent to which it is needed. These results will also act as a baseline against which you can evaluate change at a later date, using the same tools. Many schools have found the auditing process valuable in terms of identifying areas and examples of good practice on which to build.

What should the audit cover?

In line with our Wider Pedagogical Role (WPR) framework, we recommend structuring an audit around the three dimensions of TA deployment, practice and preparation.

We will highlight some specific areas within each dimension you should aim to cover in your audit, along with some suggestions about the type of tools that can be used to collect data. The examples in this chapter are based on tools used in our research, the reliability and validity of which have been tested through years of fieldwork.

There are downloadable versions of our audit tools on our website (www. maximisingtas.co.uk), along with apps you can use to set up and run your own online staff surveys. However, you should choose the auditing methods best suited to the questions you want to answer, and in this sense, our tools can be used as starting points or templates you can adapt.

You should aim to collect data that provides both an objective and subjective picture of current practice. As we have noted, it is important to get a clear sense of the extent to which: (i) what you *think* is happening in classrooms across the school matches the reality; and (ii) your perceptions of what is happening (and their effects) are shared by your staff. A further point to consider, therefore, is how different parts of the audit link together. As you will see, our tools help obtain a picture of TA deployment and practice moving from the broad school level, through the classroom level, right down to the fine detail of the pupil experience.

As we explained in the Introduction, in line with the way the responsibility for supporting the needs of lower-attaining pupils and those with SEN has shifted away from teachers towards TAs, TAs are very often handed the duty of planning, delivering and assessing curricular interventions. Based on the experiences of schools in the EDTA project, we argue there is much to be gained from a parallel review of interventions and the impact they have on pupil progress. We will cover this in later sections of the book, but for now, it is worth having in mind what a systematic evaluation of interventions (especially those delivered by TAs) would add to your audit of TA deployment.

Conducting the audit

As a school leader, you will be alert to the sensitivities involved with auditing working practices. An underlying sense of judgement sometimes accompanies such an exercise, particularly one involving TAs, who are generally unaccustomed to the type of evaluative processes more readily associated with teachers.

It is important to emphasise that any judgements that may be made on the basis of the audit findings primarily reflect the impact of historic decisions made and actions taken (or, indeed, decisions *unmade* and actions *not* taken) by the school leadership team (SLT) and teaching staff. Judgements are *not* reflections of the competency of individual TAs. If you are a headteacher new to post, these decisions will date back to your predecessor(s). The audit we describe here could form part of any wider evaluation of school processes and practice you undertake in your new leadership role.

We recommend you undertake the audit in a transparent way and that the messages about what is being judged (e.g. teachers' decisions and school processes), and what the potential impact of the audit might be, are clear to TAs. You may like to meet with your TA team and describe the rationale and audit process, gaining their cooperation and support.

TAs should not feel pressured into participating in the audit, or be made to feel it is something 'being done to them'. In particular, you should stress the audit is *not* a staff rationalisation or competency process; it is not about making judgements on the effectiveness of individual TAs and their continued employment. TAs should be made aware that they are contributing to a valuable exercise to inform whole-school improvement, and one that our work shows has considerable benefits for TAs.

Features of the audit

The deployment of TAs

You should examine TA deployment at the school level and the class (or teacher) level. The latter (which we will turn to later) is nested within the former, and so provides a view on how the effects of wider decision-making (which we consider here) play out in classrooms.

As the person responsible for setting and overseeing the whole-school vision for the overall use of TAs, you will want to know if your staff share this vision. Or, if you have a current policy on TA deployment, you will want to know the extent to which it is adhered. You should obtain a broad view of the tasks performed by TAs, in terms of the extent to which they:

- work in and away from classrooms
- lead whole classes (perhaps as part of lesson cover arrangements)
- provide pastoral support (e.g. support pupils with physical/mobility needs; facilitate social interaction; help with pupil welfare; act as mentors; manage behaviour)
- perform non-teaching tasks (e.g. prepare resources and displays; do filing; tidy up)
- prepare for, deliver and/or assess work for interventions or booster sessions
- meet with teachers to plan and prepare
- meet/liaise with parents and outside agencies.

'Time use' diary and survey

In the DISS project we used a 'work pattern diary' to obtain general information on TAs' main activities. We provided a list of the most commonly performed tasks and asked TAs to tick which tasks they carried out in 20-minute periods across one school day. We limited TAs' choices to selecting only the one or two tasks they did for the majority of each period. The data were collected anonymously.

A 'time use' analysis is powerful in terms of producing a systematic picture of not only the frequency with which TAs perform different activities, but also the time spent doing them. We recommend you conduct a similar survey over one day, if not a week. You can develop your own easy-to-complete time use diary based on the task category system we used in the DISS project, and even ask TAs to record tasks performed during unpaid hours (e.g. before/after school). A complete list of the individual activities we used, grouped into six main categories, is provided in Table 2.1.[1]

The time use diary analysis produces an objective view of school-wide TA deployment, but you may also wish to gather subjective data on the *perceptions* TAs have of the ways they work. One way to gather such information is via a questionnaire structured around the categories and tasks listed above. If you are concerned TAs might record diary data that conform to their perceptions, conduct the time use survey first. Either way, completing the questionnaire after the diary is likely to improve the accuracy of TAs' responses.

You could create a time use survey by applying a scale to some or all of the tasks, so TAs can indicate the extent to which they perform or are involved in each task. An example is shown in Table 2.2 for the tasks relating to supporting teachers and the curriculum.

The role and purpose of TAs – and teachers

The tools above allow school leaders to obtain a picture of how TAs spend their time, but it is equally important to establish an across-school view of what TAs and teachers think about the role and purpose of TAs. In Chapter 3, we cover how school leaders can develop a clearly defined role for TAs, so it is helpful to establish any misconceptions there may be about the TA role among your staff to factor into your decision-making.

A good starting place is to find out the degree to which your teachers and TAs feel their roles overlap and/or are distinct. There are several useful methods for gathering such information.

Questionnaires (especially if completed anonymously) allow individual teachers and TAs to articulate their understanding of and views about the role and purpose of TAs, and what the school expects from them. The kinds of questions relating to role clarity you need to ask include:

- What are the main responsibilities in your role as a TA in this school?
- Describe how your role as a TA differs from the role of a teacher.
- Are there any ways in which your role as a TA is similar to the role of a teacher?
- Describe the ways in which the role of the TA is distinct from your role as a teacher.
- Do you have any views about the similarities and/or differences between the teacher and TA role?
- Do you have any views about the ways in which TAs are deployed or could be deployed?

Our online staff survey app has several questions designed to capture these data quantitatively (using tick boxes and scales) and qualitatively (using open questions) from both teachers and TAs.

You might like to consider the use of focus groups. You could establish two groups (teachers and TAs) and ask each to list the criteria that define their role and contribution. To allow an open discussion, you should arrange for them to meet without SLT present. This will ensure responses are not attributable to individuals.

Table 2.1 Typical TA tasks for a school-level audit of TA deployment

1. Support for teachers/curriculum
Classroom preparation including display
Clerical support (e.g. worksheet preparation)
Give feedback to teachers
IEP development and implementation
Participate in development of lesson plans
Prepare and maintain equipment/resources
Provide advice and guidance for teachers
Record-keeping
Support and use ICT
Other *(specify)*

2. Direct learning support for pupils
Deliver lessons (covering teacher absence)
Deliver learning activities
Deliver interventions/booster programmes
Give feedback to pupils
Managing pupil behaviour
Perform pupil assessments (e.g. for SEN)
Provide specialist pupil support
Reward pupil achievement
Supervise pupils out of class
Support excluded pupils
Support for pupils to achieve learning goals
Support pupils to understand instructions
Other *(specify)*

3. Direct pastoral support for pupils
Attend to pupils' personal needs
One-to-one mentoring
First aid/pupil welfare duties
Help pupils make informed choices
Pastoral support for pupils
Provide specialist pupil support
Other *(specify)*

4. Indirect support for pupils
Interaction with parents/carers
Monitor and record pupil progress
Record-keeping
Other *(specify)*

5. Support for school (admin)
Admin tasks (e.g. ordering materials)
Carry out reception/telephone duties
Clerical/admin/general office support
Dealing with school correspondence
Facilities/premises/lettings/marketing
Financial admin (e.g. payroll, school budget)
General school administration
Liaise with agencies/external professionals
Interaction with parents/carers
Liaise between teaching and support staff
Operate attendance/pastoral systems
Participating in stock ordering/auditing
Provide advice/guidance to staff and pupils
Record-keeping
Support and use ICT
Other *(specify)*

6. Support for school (environment)
Arrange storage of stock and supplies
Assist teachers with health and safety
Other duties arising from use of premises
Carry out minor repairs
Ensure standards of cleanliness maintained
Ensure pupils' toilets properly maintained
Ensure security of premises and contents
Maintain a good working environment
Maintain and distribute stock and supplies
Maintain/check/repair equipment
Monitor and manage stock and supplies
Monitor work by outside agencies
Operate equipment
Participate in stock storage/ordering/auditing
Receive and distribute deliveries
Remove and rearrange furniture
Other *(specify)*

Table 2.2 Example of questions for TAs regarding their support for teachers/curriculum

Using the scales on the right, indicate the extent to which you are involved in the following tasks, which support teachers and the curriculum.	*Little or no involvement*		→	*High involvement*	
Classroom preparation including display	1	2	3	4	5
Clerical support (e.g. worksheet preparation)	1	2	3	4	5
Give feedback to teachers	1	2	3	4	5
IEP development and implementation	1	2	3	4	5
Participate in development of lesson plans	1	2	3	4	5
Prepare and maintain equipment/resources	1	2	3	4	5
Provide advice and guidance for teachers	1	2	3	4	5
Record-keeping	1	2	3	4	5
Support and use ICT	1	2	3	4	5
Other *(specify)*	1	2	3	4	5

Case studies

Consulting staff 1

To encourage openness and honesty, teachers in one primary school interviewed each other's TA. TAs were asked the same set of questions. They appreciated being asked for their views. Teachers described the process as 'very revealing', as the process uncovered a wide range of perceptions and ideas about the TA role. The consultation showed a lack of a common understanding of the TA role, and initiated a much-needed discussion about how to establish consistency.

Consulting staff 2

SLT in another primary school had become aware of variations across the school in terms of how TAs were utilised and wanted to ensure greater consistency. The deputy headteacher led separate sessions with teachers and TAs. Staff had to work through a list of statements about TAs' duties and decide if each was a task TAs should do, may sometimes do, or should not be expected to do. (See Appendix 1 for the list of tasks.) SLT then used the results of this exercise to create a whole-school agreement. The deputy headteacher explains:

> We decided to put this agreement on our school website, so that everyone – parents, governors and staff – is clear about how important our TAs are and the kind of things that they do in class. It is clear from lesson observations that TAs are being used as per this agreement. What is even better to hear is how happy and reinvigorated our TAs now feel.

Our research and on-going work with schools has uncovered worrying evidence about which members of staff have the responsibility for pupils with SEN (Webster and Blatchford 2014; Webster et al. 2013). There is a view among some secondary school teachers that meeting the needs of pupils with learning difficulties is the responsibility of the Learning Support department, where TAs are based and where pupils go to do interventions. Where the common practice was to assign a TA to a particular pupil (typically those who had a Statement of SEN), it led to teachers passing the responsibility for instruction or differentiating material to TAs, or assuming TAs would take this on – which they did.

Given the well-documented association between TAs and pupils with SEN, the issue of who has responsibility for pupils with SEN should be addressed in your audit. Ask teachers and TAs what they perceive as their respective roles and responsibilities in relation to the school's provision for pupils with SEN. This is best achieved by neutrally worded, open-ended questions you could add to a survey or ask your focus groups. For example:

- How would you describe your role in meeting the needs of pupils with SEN?
- If you are a TA, what do you identify as teachers' main duties for meeting the needs of pupils with SEN?
- If you are a teacher, what do you identify as TAs' main duties for meeting the needs of pupils with SEN?
- What are your views on how effectively the school meets the learning needs of pupils with SEN?

The auditing process will produce two sets of data – from teachers and TAs – reflecting:

- teachers' and TAs' understanding of, and views about, their respective roles
- teachers' understanding of, and views about, the TA role
- TAs' understanding of, and views about, their own role
- the extent to which teacher and TA roles are distinct
- teachers' and TAs' understanding of their own and one another's role and responsibilities regarding pupils with SEN.

These data can be analysed and put together with your own understanding of the role and purpose of TAs. This might necessitate surveying the members of your SLT and your SENCo (if he/she is not a member of the SLT). Our online staff survey app has this facility.

We are aware of some school leaders who have made use of official documentation that formally set out the teacher and TA roles in order to inform their audit. The Qualified Teacher Status (QTS) standards, standards for obtaining HLTA status, and TA role profiles produced by local authorities (which outline the key responsibilities and entry level requirements for TAs at three or four different levels) are useful for establishing the demarcation between the teacher and TA roles.

Case study

Including TAs in the decision-making process

Senior leaders held a meeting with TAs to introduce the school's plan to develop their role. The school planned to review and clarify roles of TAs on different grades, and amend job descriptions as necessary. There was an open forum for questions, many of which revealed anxieties about job security and the implications of the new job descriptions. Some TAs were reluctant to move outside their comfort zone of working with familiar year groups. There were concerns too about the 'finding out process' SLT were embarking on, in terms of the purpose of observations of TAs at work.

To allay these understandable anxieties, SLT offered on-going reassurance and focused on the positives for TAs, in terms of skills development, and the wider educational aims; for example, whether it was the interventions that TAs led that were ineffective, not TAs themselves.

SLT kept TAs informed about the process and responded to questions as they arose. Moreover, TAs were included in the decision-making process. They were asked for their views on which year groups they would like to work in and surveyed about their skills and experience – all of which fed into SLT's decisions about allocating roles.

The provision mapping process identified three types of TA role: HLTA; intervention specialists; and classroom support. To assign individuals to roles, SLT drew on findings from a skills audit, observations and consultation with TAs. The aim was to assign TA roles based on their skills, expertise and preferences where possible.

TA deployment at the classroom level

As part of your audit, you must also obtain a detailed picture of the current models of TA deployment at the classroom level. In our experience, this is where the most revealing data about TA deployment will be found. Yet the TA's role in a lesson is only one side of the coin. The role of the teacher must also be considered because, as we have explained, decisions they make about TAs have implications for the ways in which teachers organise their *own* work (e.g. in terms of which groups of pupils they work with).

Teachers involved in the EDTA study told us they found the auditing process productive as it provoked them into thinking about the models of classroom organisation they used, and in many ways had taken for granted. Information on how teachers deploy TAs helps them to reflect on and change their classroom practice.

We recommend you gather subjective views from individuals (e.g. via a survey) and a more objective method, specifically classroom observations. We will consider the use of both methods, starting with ways to survey your staff.

SURVEYING TEACHERS AND TAs

In the EDTA study we used an audit survey to gather subjective data from teachers and TAs on their perceptions of how they spent their time in the classroom. The questions we asked can be seen in the top half of Table 2.3. For both questions, teachers and TAs were asked to consider the occasions when they worked alongside each other in the classroom, and to estimate the proportion of their time they spent in the contexts listed (e.g. working with small groups). Questions regarding work away from the classroom (e.g. in a shared area, corridor or a specialist provision) were asked only to TAs. These can be seen in the bottom half of Table 2.3.

Teachers and TAs in the EDTA project were asked to estimate how they spent their time over a typical week. To address the fact that many TAs work part-time, you might instead ask your TAs to consider their deployment over a full day, or even a lesson. An editable version of the survey in Table 2.3 is available to download from our website.

There are other ways to obtain these data; for example, by using a ranking system. Ask teachers and TAs to think about their most recent lesson and get them to rank the time spent in the listed contexts; from the context they spent the most time working in, to the one they spent the least time working in. Our online staff survey app takes this approach and produces useful data for school leaders.

Table 2.3 Example of survey questions on deployment in and away from classrooms

Working in the classroom (to be completed by teachers and TAs)

During a typical school week, estimate the proportion of time (as a %) that you spend doing the following. Only provide a percentage score for item 6 if you are a TA. Ensure that your percentages add up to 100%.

1) Working with a pupil one-to-one	%
2) Working with a small group (up to 5 pupils)	%
3) Working with a larger group (between 6 and 10 pupils)	%
4) Roving the classroom	%
5) Leading the class	%
6) (*TAs only*) Listening to teacher talk to the class	%
7) Other (please specify)	%
Total	100%

During a typical school week, estimate the proportion of time (as a %) that you spend doing the following. Ensure that your percentages add up to 100%.

1) Supporting higher-attaining pupils	%
2) Supporting average-attaining pupils	%
3) Supporting lower-attaining pupils	%
4) Supporting pupils identified as having SEN (e.g. those with a Statement or EHCP)	%
5) Supporting mixed attainment groups	%
Total	100%

Working away from the classroom (to be completed by TAs only)

During a typical school week, estimate the proportion of time (as a %) that you spend doing the following. Ensure that your percentages add up to 100%

1) Working with a pupil one-to-one (e.g. leading an intervention)	%
2) Working with a group of pupils (e.g. leading an intervention)	%
3) Working with pupil(s) in a pastoral/welfare context (e.g. mentoring; physio)	%
4) Preparing, planning and/or assessing pupil work (including for interventions)	%
5) Doing administrative tasks (e.g. photocopying or filing for teachers; display)	%
6) Other (please specify)	%
Total	100%

During a typical school week, estimate the proportion of time (as a %) that you spend doing the following. Ensure that your percentages add up to 100%.

1) Supporting higher-attaining pupils	%
2) Supporting average-attaining pupils	%
3) Supporting lower-attaining pupils	%
4) Supporting pupils identified as having SEN (e.g. those with a Statement or EHCP)	%
5) Supporting mixed attainment groups	%
Total	100%

Case study

A process of 'finding out'

The teachers in one primary school conducted a small-scale audit of their TAs, with the aim of ensuring that the teachers made best use of the TAs' time. The teachers drew up a comprehensive list of the tasks TAs performed (e.g. supporting an individual pupil; working with a small group; roving around the classroom; preparing resources, etc.) in different parts of the lesson. TAs were asked to rate on a five-point scale how often they thought they spent time doing those tasks (e.g. very frequently, frequently, sometimes, rarely or not at all).

The teachers developed this checklist into a simple observation schedule, which the TAs completed for one another. Particular attention was paid to the TA role during teacher input, group work and plenary.

The TA-completed checklists and observations were followed up with discussions between each teacher-TA pair, in which the TAs were asked about the different tasks they did during the lesson. This in turn led to a conversation about how the TAs could make best use of their time in lessons. The TAs identified the following: making notes on teacher input for later use with groups; monitoring pupils' reactions for signs of understanding or confusion; and encouraging pupils to contribute to class discussions.

Surveying teachers and TAs can produce detailed classroom-level data to examine alongside school-level data on the purpose and role of TAs, confirming and/or contradicting the overall picture presented by these subjective views. However, to add an extra layer of meaning to the audit process, it is necessary to supplement these data with data from classroom observations.

OBSERVING TEACHERS AND TAs

We are not always our own most reliable witness. It is human nature to overestimate and underestimate how we spend our time. For this reason, we strongly recommend conducting observations of TAs in action throughout the school, working in classrooms alongside teachers, and away from classrooms with individual pupils and groups.

The value of using lesson observations in order to generate a deeper understanding of classroom processes is well known, and indeed, the DISS project and the MAST study both relied heavily on the use of observational data in order to build a systematic, moment-by-moment description of how TAs and teachers were deployed in classrooms and the roles they undertook. It was in the light of the findings from the DISS project lesson observations in particular that we were initially able to make sense of the troubling results on pupil progress.

We provide a simplified version of the tried and tested lesson observation schedule used in the EDTA project in Table 2.4, which we present as a worked example to make clear its intended use. We have completed the sheet using data from an actual classroom observation conducted as part of our research. A blank version of the observation pro forma can be downloaded from our website.

The lesson observation schedule is designed to help you not only derive a clear systematic picture of how TAs are deployed in classrooms, what roles they undertake and for how long, but further, to obtain an understanding of how teachers make use of TAs (especially with regard to meeting the needs of lower-attaining pupils and those with SEN) and how their own pedagogical practice is affected by the presence and deployment of a TA.

We suggest observations are conducted by senior members of your change team (i.e. SLT) and that you observe all of your TAs at least once. While learning walks are helpful for gaining a sense of what is happening in and away from classrooms, we strongly recommend you observe lessons in their entirety.

The process for completing the observation schedule is straightforward. With reference to Table 2.4, you will notice the schedule has been designed to allow a TA's activities to be recorded on a minute-by-minute basis over a one-hour lesson.

The second column is for you to log the phase of the lesson in progress (e.g. teacher's main input, main learning task and plenary). A point raised by our research concerns the fact that the way in which lessons are structured affects the TA's role. For example, TAs often spend the teacher input stage listening to the teacher – in effect, being part of the class audience; during the main learning task, they mostly work with individuals or groups; and while the teacher is leading the plenary, TAs often gather in books and resources or tidy the room. This is by no means to say this is what goes on in every lesson in every classroom, but it is, in our experience, commonplace and worth drawing to your attention. The rationale for the 'Lesson part' column is to help you obtain a picture of the TA role during key parts of the lesson. These data may reveal broad patterns of TA deployment across the school.

The five columns grouped under the heading 'Predominant activity of TA' are used to summarise the main role the TA had during each minute of the lesson; that is, what he/she did for 30 seconds or more (please note: these 30 seconds do not have to be consecutive). You could summarise TA activity every second minute if you prefer, using the alternately shaded rows as a guide (e.g. indicate the predominant TA activity over a two-minute, rather than one-minute block). However, for your analyses to be meaningful, you will need to be consistent across all observations.

The total number of ticks per column should be entered in the bottom row (Total ✓). This can be converted to a percentage of the total per observation to summarise the main activities of the TA (Summary). In the worked example in Table 2.4, the TA worked with pupils on either a one-to-one or group basis for the majority of the time (53 per cent cumulatively), and listened to the teacher teach for a third of the lesson (35 per cent). Such data become very meaningful when aggregated across a greater number of observations.

The four wider columns on the right of the schedule allow you to add qualitative notes on the pupil(s) with whom the TA works (TA-supported pupil(s)) and any evidence of the extent to which the tasks the TA supports pupils with have been differentiated, or are different, from the tasks undertaken by the rest of the class.

General notes on the 'teacher's role' and interactions with pupils at significant points in the lesson are also helpful, as they will reveal similarities and differences

Table 2.4 Worked example of lesson observation schedule, adapted from version used in the EDTA project

Date: 17/09/15 **Teacher:** R. Lee (RL) **TA:** T. Allen (TA) **Class/Year:** 5

Lesson details: (topic/objectives) LITERACY. Narratives. *Learning objective – to write opposite character descriptions (i.e. Dracula and victim; superhero and villain)*

Time (minutes)	Lesson part *	With pupil one-to-one	With group of pupils	Roving classroom	Listening to teacher teach	Other task (tidying/admin)	TA-supported pupil(s) (name, attainment level, SEN status)	Task differentiation for TA-supported pupils	Comments on teacher's role	Features of TA-to-pupil talk
1	1				✓		TA sat on carpet with J (SEN Support) & B (EHCP for ASD)		RL sets talk partner starter activity: words to describe your partner's appearance	Prompts to focus attention (pre-emptive)
2	1				✓					
3	1				✓					
4	1				✓					
5	1				✓					
6	1		✓				TA works with J & B for starter activity		RL observes class as they do talk partner task	Lots of TA talk. Little chance for J & B to interact with each other
7	1		✓							
8	1		✓							
9	1				✓				RL gives whole class input	
10	1				✓		TA sat with J & B			TA repeating RL's talk to J & B – questions, key words
11	1				✓					
12	1				✓					Prompt B to put up hand to answer RL's question
13	1				✓					
14	1				✓					
15	1				✓					Mostly passive; not interacting with pupils
16	1				✓					
17	1				✓					
18	1				✓					

Table 2.4 continued

Date: 17/09/15 **Teacher:** R. Lee (RL) **TA:** T. Allen (TA)

Class/Year: 5

Lesson details: (topic/objectives) LITERACY. Narratives. Learning objective – to write opposite character descriptions (i.e. Dracula and victim; superhero and villain)

Predominant activity of TA

Time (minutes)	Lesson part *	With pupil one-to-one	With group of pupils	Roving classroom	Listening to teacher teach	Other task (tidying/admin)	TA-supported pupil(s) (name, attainment level, SEN status)	Task differentiation for TA-supported pupils	Comments on teacher's role	Features of TA-to-pupil talk
19	T		✓				TA works with 4 lower-attaining pupils on Red table: J, B, C & D.	RL tells TA that pupils on Red table need only describe one character – Dracula.	RL works with 5 higher-attaining pupils (5 mins). Use of high order questioning.	Clear explanation of task. Gives examples of adjectives. Checks understanding: 'What are adjectives?'
20	T		✓							
21	T		✓							
22	T		✓							Some open questions used, not well targeted.
23	T		✓				TA sits next to B			
24	T		✓						RL roves class, checks pupils are on-task & progressing. Roves to all tables but Red table	
25	T		✓							Procedural talk: tells pupils to underline title, write date, make a start.
26	T		✓							
27	T		✓							
28	T		✓				As pupils begin task, TA withdraws from Red table. Roves between 2 average-attaining tables	Average-attaining pupils have to describe 2 characters		Promotes independence when asked for a spelling: 'How can you find out for yourself?'
29	T			✓						
30	T		✓	✓					RL working with pair of pupils on average attaining table	
31	T		✓	✓						
32	T		✓	✓	✓					Task-related: 'Come on. We need to get this done!', etc.
33	T				✓				RL talks to class to restate instructions	
34	T				✓					
35	T				✓					
36	T		✓				TA at Red table, checking progress. Pupils make slow start		RL uses laptop (3 mins)	
37	T		✓							
38	T		✓							

			✓				TA gives one-to-one support to B who is off-task/disengaged		RL with average attaining pupils. Evaluative questions: 'How would you feel if you met this scary character?'	TA repeats lots of closed questions. Little thinking time given for B to respond.
39	T		✓							
40	T		✓							
41	T		✓							
42	T		✓							
43	T		✓				TA draws J into interaction as he is having similar problem understanding abstract concept		RL at higher-attaining table: marking work, giving feedback	TA uses leading statements. Some spoon-feeding: 'We could say that Dracula has a long black cloak.'
44	T		✓							
45	T		✓							
46	T		✓							
47	T		✓						RL at Red table. Asks C and D to read their sentences out to her. Praises efforts	
48	T		✓							
49	T		✓							
50	T				✓		Supporting J & B			TA talks to RL. Task-related talk. TA seems keen that J & B have written something before end of lesson
51	T				✓					
52	T				✓					
53	T				✓					
54	P	✓	✓							
55	P		✓							
56	P	✓					Collects in pupils' books		RL brings task to a close	
57	P	✓								
58	P			✓			Listens in to RL's plenary		RL leads plenary	
59	P			✓						
60	P			✓						
Total ✓		6	26	4	21	3				
Summary		10%	43%	7%	35%	5%				

* Key for lesson part: I = Teacher's main input T = Main learning task P = Plenary

between the two roles. You can use the time intervals in the left-hand column to make these notes at concurrent intervals.

Those who are confident using this kind of observation method may wish to use another observation schedule to collect concurrent data about the prominent role of the teacher at one- or two-minute intervals. In this way, you can perform an analysis that allows you to make a comparison of teacher and TA activities in the classroom, as we did in the EDTA project (Blatchford et al. 2012a).

The last column on the observation schedule (*Features of TA-to-pupil talk*) can be used to record key features of the TA's talk in line with the time points from the observation. This is also why noting the lesson part is useful, as you can generate a fairly reliable picture of the TA role and the types of TA talk at different phases of the lesson, for example, what the TA says to pupils when sitting beside them during the teacher's main input, or when working with a group during the main learning task. These notes can be made with reference to the directory of the common features of TA talk shown in Table 2.5. TA-to-pupil interaction is covered in detail in Chapter 5.

We strongly recommend you observe TAs in two other contexts, if relevant to current deployment practice in your school. First, you should observe TAs when they lead classes. The DISS study revealed some schools used TAs as part of their arrangements for covering planned and unplanned teacher absence, and also to free up time for teachers' planning, preparation and assessment time. These greater responsibilities represent a significant development in the history of the TA role, as they bring the TA to the front of the class in ways not seen before. As part of your audit, it is essential for you to know how effectively TAs who are given this role manage classrooms and deliver lessons. The observation schedule in Table 2.4 can easily be used to collect these data.

The second context in which you should observe TAs is when they are working away from the classroom, delivering interventions with individuals and groups. Again, you can use the observation schedule to collect these data; however, our experience of observations of this kind suggests it will be much more meaningful for you to take qualitative notes, paying particular attention to TAs' interactions with pupils.

The practice of TAs

A fine-grained description of TA–pupil interaction gets to the heart of what is central to all learning. Much of what TAs do in school involves working with pupils, yet we have found these important interactions represent a 'black box', the lid of which is rarely, if ever, lifted. This is not to suggest that TA–pupil interactions are secretive, but merely to draw attention to a feature of classroom life that has long been taken for granted.

Given the centrality of interactions to learning outcomes, your audit should aim to provide a better understanding of the nature of TA-to-pupil talk, and the ways in which these interactions reflect the wider deployment and preparation decisions that shape TAs' work.

For the purposes of the DISS project, we conducted a rigorous analysis of TA-to-pupil (and teacher-to-pupil) dialogue from transcriptions of recordings (Radford et al. 2012). The findings were extremely revealing, but this level of analysis may well be impractical for a school-based TA audit. An analysis of TA–pupil interactions adds a rich layer of detail that can often go undetected in an observation (e.g. because the observer is positioned too far away from the TA, or there is interference from general classroom noise).

An audit of TA–pupil talk can be nested within (that is, form part of) the classroom observations described above. The observation schedule (Table 2.4) has space in which you can write notes about TA-to-pupil talk *in situ*. But even better than this, in our experience, is to make notes based on recordings of TA talk made during lessons, which can be played back as many times as you need. In the DISS project, we successfully used a digital voice recorder to capture TA talk unobtrusively.[2] The vast majority of TAs, who were often (and understandably) tentative about being recorded at first, told us afterwards they quickly forgot about the recorder and spoke and acted as they would have had they not been wearing it. There is more on how to make and analyse audio and video recordings of TAs at work in this book's sister publication, *The Teaching Assistant's Guide To Effective Interaction: How to Maximise Your Impact* (Bosanquet, Radford and Webster 2016).

As previously mentioned, you must be sensitive to the concerns of TAs who may feel 'over-scrutinised'. We cannot overstate the need for reassurance and transparency in the conduct of the audit.

Features of TA-to-pupil talk

The skilled and experienced practitioner will already know the features and purposes of classroom talk (e.g. prompting, questioning and so on), but we have drawn on our research and the literature on effective teaching to provide a directory of the common features of TA talk. This directory, shown in Table 2.5, provides descriptions and examples of the types of talk to which we recommend you are attentive, not least because some of these types of talk have been shown through our research to be less effective than others, in terms of their influence on pupil outcomes.

The directory should be considered indicative, rather than definitive; there may well be features you wish to add. Also, we do not mean to imply certain types of talk are always ineffective; for example, there are occasions when asking a closed question is entirely appropriate if the aim is to elicit simple recall. The purpose of setting out the examples is to draw your attention to the fact that advancing pupil learning is impeded by the overuse of less effective types of talk. Our research shows TAs tend not to take the opportunities in their interactions with pupils to ask higher-order questions, and this is principally because they are unaware of how to make use of the cues that invite such talk. TAs' routine use of spoon-feeding and leading statements, rather than encouraging pupils to think for themselves, encourages dependency.

Additionally, there are overarching features of talk, such as how TAs pace their talk and how they handle pupil responses that you may also wish to consider; for example, are pupils given adequate time to respond to a question?

In line with our advice on observations, you should pay attention to TA talk in relation to instances where TAs lead classes and where they deliver intervention sessions away from the classroom.

Table 2.5 Features of TA-to-pupil talk with examples

1 Closing down pupil talk	
Spoon-feeding (supplying answers)	The answer is a thousand.
Leading statements	The answer starts with a 'th' … 'thou' … 'thousan' …
Lower-order/closed questions	Which of these shapes is a square?
	Who wrote this book?
2 Prioritising task completion	
Statements/prompts emphasising the need to complete the task	We've got to get this done by the end of the lesson. Come on. There's only five minutes of the lesson left before break.
3 Opening up pupil talk	
Statements to motivate; promote cognitive focus/engagement with task	You need to think about the words that you can use in your story. They need to be creative words that make up layers of meaning.
Higher-order/open questions	Can you tell me why that shape is called a square and why that shape is called a rectangle? How are you going to solve this problem?
Probing a pupil's response	Where do we start when we see this kind of sum? Have you seen one before? What do you mean when you describe the prince as 'posh'?
4 Providing explanations (with clarity and accuracy)	
Explaining a process	To divide 108 by 6, first note that 6 times 10 equals 60. So you subtract 60 from 108 and are left with 48. Then you tackle the smaller problem of 48 divided by 6.
Explaining a concept	The water cycle involves the sun heating the Earth's surface water and causing the surface water to evaporate.
Explaining an instruction	We have to put one spatula of copper sulphate in the beaker and then measure the temperature.
5 Drawing on prior learning	
Linking content of the current lesson to prior learning (e.g. from a previous lesson)	To help you, think about what we did last lesson when we were drawing two-dimensional shapes. What did we say 25% was equivalent to yesterday when we did fractions?
6 Managing pupil behaviour	
Reacting to off-task behaviour (e.g. reprimands)	If you are doodling, you're not listening. That tells me you're not doing the right thing.
Pre-emptive statements to prevent the likelihood of off-task behaviour	Put that away please. Why don't you come and sit here, so you're not tempted to mess about.
Focusing pupil attention	If you keep being good, I'll give you a sticker. Are you listening to the teacher? Face the board.

Case study

TA observations

Given the sizable task of addressing TA deployment at the school level, one secondary SENCo made some quick wins by addressing TAs' less effective types of talk. Drawing on the DISS project results, the SENCo developed a list of 'pitfalls' he noticed TAs unintentionally fell into in their interactions with pupils. These included: separation from classmates; unnecessary dependence; interference with teacher engagement; loss of personal control and provocation of poor behaviour. 'Things,' he said, 'that we could change very quickly in the way we approach things [and] avoid those pitfalls.'

The preparedness of TAs and teachers

The final area your audit should cover concerns the training received by TAs and teachers, and TAs' day-to-day preparation. Surveying the preparedness of your staff will help ascertain the extent to which TAs are briefed and made aware of their role in lessons, and how well equipped they are to carry out what teachers ask of them.

Training

It is worth collecting comprehensive data on TAs' training and qualifications in order to build a complete picture of the courses they have completed and particular areas of knowledge and skills they possess. Given the wide variation in training routes and high number of courses available to TAs, we have found the most effective method of collecting these data is to ask TAs to list any professional qualifications and training they have received, including on-the-job training.

In our experience, preparedness can be a sensitive area of enquiry, so we recommend collecting data on day-to-day preparation anonymously, via a survey (more of which below). However, as data on TAs' training and qualifications are less sensitive, we advise collecting this information separately. Asking TAs to provide their names is necessary, as you will want to know their individual skills sets.

As a result of this process, it may become immediately clear that some individuals are inadequately prepared for teaching particular subjects. This will inform your decision-making about the appropriateness of the roles given to, and demands put on, certain TAs, and what you do about it (e.g. up-skilling or redeployment).

Day-to-day preparation

In terms of TAs' day-to-day preparation, the best people to ask, of course, are TAs. However, schools we have worked with have found obtaining teachers' perceptions of TA preparedness is also very valuable. Therefore, you should give teachers and TAs the same survey questions, so you can compare the responses between the two groups and expose any differences or similarities in their perceptions. You will need to know about the opportunities for teachers and TAs to meet, and the nature and quality of information that flows between them, in relation to support in everyday classrooms and the delivery of intervention programmes. Additionally, it is helpful to have a sense of how TAs acquire the subject and instructional knowledge required for them to provide effective support.

Our online staff survey asks questions on these particular topics to teachers and TAs. School leaders in the MITA programme use the online survey and many find the results on preparedness to be the most revealing of all, with surprising and not-so-surprising results coming to light.

A basic one-page version of preparedness questions, amended from ones used in the EDTA project audit, is shown in Table 2.6. An editable version of the one-page survey can be downloaded from our website. The online survey is more thorough, however, the questions cannot be edited.

It is important to make teachers and TAs aware that completion of the survey requires making a 'best fit' judgement. Each set of statements is ordered with what we regard as the least effective practice at the top, and the most effective practice at the bottom. We acknowledge that the statements reflect broad circumstances and that the actual situations experienced by individuals are likely to be more complex than those described in the scenarios. Therefore, respondents should select the response that represents their most common experience.

Other audit questions to consider

TEACHERS' PREPAREDNESS TO WORK WITH AND MANAGE TAs

As we argued earlier, your teachers may also be inadequately prepared to work with and manage TAs. Therefore, it is important for you to discover the extent to which teachers feel prepared or adequately trained to organise TAs and their work. You could explore this via a teacher focus group.

TEACHERS' KNOWLEDGE OF SEN

Another element of preparedness, very much bound up with TAs' preparedness for the roles and tasks given to them by teachers, concerns teachers' knowledge of SEN. This includes the identification and understanding of the most common types of SEN and the knowledge of and skill in using pedagogic strategies suited to pupils with those needs. The audit should be used to elicit this information. You may find that, in line with the DISS project findings, a patchy picture emerges in terms of the quality of training teachers have received. The 2014 SEN reforms have raised the profile and importance of this area of school practice, so should your audit reveal deficiencies in teachers' competence and confidence to meet the needs of pupils with SEN, you will need to respond. We discuss the implications of the SEN reforms in Chapter 3.

Table 2.6 Example of survey questions on preparedness

1 Opportunity for teacher–TA pre-lesson communication	✓

1) No opportunity/time to communicate before lessons
2) Communication before lessons is brief and *ad hoc*
3) TA comes in early/stays behind after school to meet with teacher for briefing
4) Teacher and TA have scheduled time to meet (e.g. time for which TA is paid)

2 Quality of preparation for TA (teachers' lesson plans)	✓

1) TA goes into lessons blind. No lesson plan provided
2) TA given lesson plan. No specific information about TA role given
3) TA given lesson plan. Limited information about TA role given (e.g. names of pupils to support)
4) TA given lesson plan. Specific information about TA role given (e.g. specific objectives/outcomes)

3 Opportunity for teacher–TA post-lesson communication	✓

1) No opportunity/time to communicate after lessons
2) Communication after lessons is brief and *ad hoc*
3) TA comes in early/stays behind after school to meet with teacher for debriefing
4) Teacher and TA have scheduled time to meet (e.g. time for which TA is paid)

4 Quality of TA feedback to teachers (written/verbal)	✓

1) TA does not feed information back to teachers
2) TA feeds back basic information (e.g. 'task completed'; 'pupils on-task')
3) TA feeds back detailed information (e.g. specific problems with/progress towards learning goals)

5 Preparation for interventions: guidance from teachers	✓

1) TA plans and prepares interventions, with very little/no input from teachers
2) TA plans and prepares interventions, with some general guidance from teachers
3) TA plans and prepares interventions, with substantive, detailed guidance from teachers

6 Feedback on interventions: quality of TA's feedback to teachers (written/verbal)	✓

1) TA does not feed information back to teachers
2) TA feeds back basic information (e.g. 'task completed'; 'pupils on-task')
3) TA feeds back detailed information (e.g. specific problems with/progress towards learning goals)

7 Subject knowledge	✓

1) TA gains subject knowledge by tuning in to teacher delivery (e.g. as part of class audience)
2) TA gains subject knowledge from lesson plans and/or schemes of work
3) TA gains subject knowledge via *ad hoc* communication with teacher
4) TA gains subject knowledge via substantive briefing/training from teacher
5) TA has significant level of subject knowledge via specific training (e.g. TA has degree in subject)

8 Instructional knowledge	✓

1) TA gains instructional knowledge by tuning in to teacher delivery (e.g. as part of class audience)
2) TA gains instructional knowledge from lesson plans and/or schemes of work
3) TA gains instructional knowledge via *ad hoc* communication with teacher
4) TA gains instructional knowledge via substantive briefing/training from teacher
5) TA has significant level of instructional knowledge via specific training (e.g. TA has QTS)

PERFORMANCE MANAGEMENT FOR TAs

There are structured annual performance management procedures in place for teachers, but many schools do not have as rigorous a process in place for TAs. As a result of reforming the way in which TAs are deployed and prepared in your school, you ought to put in place an on-going process to review TA performance and identify any training needs. A necessary component of your audit will be to consider what performance review processes you already have in place – formal and informal – and consider how these could be made more systematic, rigorous and relevant to individuals.

PUPIL VOICE

We have chosen not to include input from pupils in our recommendations concerning the audit. However, you may feel it is important to seek their opinions or consult them on proposed changes to TA deployment. Furthermore, you may wish to involve parents, particularly those of children with SEN, who are likely to be most affected by changes to existing practice. Alison Ekins' book, *The Changing Face of Special Educational Needs* (2015), contains helpful suggestions on consulting pupils and parents.

Summary

The aim of this chapter has been to build on the questions raised in the book so far, and to provide you with the tools to conduct an audit of current practice. Any process of change in any organisation must begin from a position of clarity in terms of how things are presently. In other words, you need to know what to change and the extent of change needed before you can begin to make improvements. This will ensure resources are targeted effectively and the whole process is efficient.

Finally, once the process is set up, the auditing tools can be used again at a later date to help you evaluate the extent of change; essentially providing you with an 'after' picture to set alongside the 'before' picture. We recommend you perform some form of evaluation at regular intervals, so any changes that are not effective can be altered; for example, by using observations or monitoring surveys. The apps on our website automate parts of the monitoring process and provide useful data for tracking your journey.

Notes

1   For further information, see Blatchford et al. (2008).
2   Digital voice recorders are relatively inexpensive items that can be purchased from online retailers for as little as £20 each. We have found using a tie-clip microphone plugged into the recorder not only makes for a better quality recording, but is also more discreet; the recorder can be hidden away in a pocket. Tie-clip microphones can be purchased online for less than £5.

Chapter 3

Defining your vision

Introduction

Defining a clear vision is the most important strategic step in maximising the impact of teaching assistants. In this chapter, we consider the process of introducing school-wide change and what makes change 'stick'. We will challenge your perceptions about the role of TAs, the ways they are deployed and the impact they have on pupil outcomes, and ask you to consider a fundamental question about the role, purpose and contribution of TAs in your school. Here, we get to the heart of why the process of rethinking and reforming your use of TAs is key to unlocking their potential.

We make reference to the SEN Code of Practice and the wider political landscape (as at summer 2015) in order to demonstrate the incentives and opportunities there are for schools and the spaces within which leaders can think about alternative roles for TAs.

Stewardship versus leadership

Writing in the *Harvard Business Review*, Beer and Nohria (2000) suggest that up to 70 per cent of change initiatives within organisations fail. The main reason for this can be summed up in terms of how leadership can give way to stewardship. Leaders define the strategic vision and put the structures in place to allow other members of the organisation to play their role in the drive towards that vision. Certainly in larger organisations (academy chains, school federations and many secondary schools would fall into this category), leadership is something of an 'arms-length' activity. However, the day-to-day tasks of solving problems as they arise can often get in the way. This is stewardship. The more leaders get drawn into stewardship, the more likely it is they get drawn away from their strategic focus. This can be a gradual drift and happens without the leader really noticing.

In schools, the myriad (and seemingly ever-changing) number of things to which leaders need to attend can feel overwhelming. In such cases, it is entirely understandable why some school leaders are concerned about the lack of opportunity to engage in the kinds of activities they know will drive up standards, because administrative tasks and deadlines get in the way. If you are a school leader, the key thing to bear in mind is this: while you can arrange things so that others (for example, middle leaders) attend to day-to-day problems, you cannot delegate top-level organisational leadership.

'Leadership, leadership and still more leadership'

Stepping away from the fire-fighting and committing time and effort to defining a clear vision for your TA workforce is a critical initial step for school leaders. The MITA approach is loosely underpinned by a framework developed by Harvard Business School academic, John Kotter. Kotter's (1995) framework describes an eight-step process to bringing about and embedding lasting and transformative change within an organisation. Kotter (1996) says in any organisation, the driving force behind the process of bringing about change is 'leadership, leadership, and still more leadership'.

It is worth listing Kotter's eight steps, as we will use them as markers in our description of the MITA process in this chapter:

Step 1   Establish a sense of urgency
Step 2   Create a guiding coalition
Step 3   Develop a clear vision
Step 4   Communicate the vision
Step 5   Empower people to act on the vision
Step 6   Create short-term wins
Step 7   Consolidate and build on gains
Step 8   Institutionalise the change

The first step is to establish a sense of urgency; a sense that something must be done about a particular issue. The fact you are reading this book suggests you are already on the first rung of Kotter's ladder. Your sense of urgency may well have been ratcheted up a notch or two having read this far in; and it may increase further as you examine the realities of the situation in your school on the basis of the results of your audit.

This first step also involves identifying opportunities. As far as the MITA process is concerned, this means taking a close look at things within the current educational milieu that can inform your vision-setting.

Framing change

At the end of Chapter 1, we said that the MITA process is no substitute for addressing how your school meets the needs of pupils with SEN. It is important to decouple questions about the use of TAs and how schools meet the needs of pupils with SEN and those at risk of underachievement. This way of thinking is a core principle underpinning the MITA process and it avoids loading unrealistic expectations on what it can achieve.

There are two questions school leaders need to think about over and above efforts to rethink the role of TAs: (i) how does your school ensure high quality teaching for children and young people with SEN?; and (ii) how does your school organise and integrate curriculum interventions and catch-up programmes for those falling behind?

School leaders need to answer these questions independently of solutions that directly involve installing TAs as an informal teaching resource on a routine basis. Let us be clear: we think TAs can have a role in working with lower-attaining pupils and those with SEN. But in order for these pupils to get the high quality pedagogical input they require, the work of TAs must be *part of* a wider set of provisions, such as support from specialist teachers, more time with class teachers, assistive technology and peer supports. The research evidence should be sufficient to compel us to realise TA support can no longer be the default, *or only*, option for struggling pupils. Indeed, this way of organising provision for pupils with the highest level of need has now been shown to be a discredited model.

The two questions above are not addressed in detail in this book, but they do help us define the territory in which we can answer questions about how we ensure teachers organise classrooms effectively with TAs present, and how we might maximise TAs' contributions. We recognise schools need to work within given parameters exerted by external influences. So let us take a look at the forces impacting on schools and, as Kotter says, identify the opportunities that might help us achieve our goal.

The SEN Code of Practice: 'Underpinned by high quality teaching'

Since the first edition of this book in 2013, the teacher's role and responsibilities have become more tightly focussed in relation to meeting the needs of children and young people with SEN. A founding principle of the new SEN Code of Practice is that 'special educational provision is underpinned by high quality teaching and is compromised by anything less' (DfE/DoH 2015, p25). This notion of compromise seems to have been informed by findings from the DISS and MAST studies (though we cannot be certain). Either way, the Code of Practice is expressly clear on lines of accountability: 'Teachers are responsible and accountable for the progress and development of the pupils in their class, including where pupils access support from teaching assistants or specialist staff' (DfE/DoH 2015, p.99).

Based on what we know from the research, we might replace the word 'including' in the paragraph above, with the word 'especially'.

As for TAs themselves, the Code of Practice makes no mention of their responsibilities or accountabilities in relation to pupils with SEN. This is an important point, because it means that schools should not act in ways (intentionally or otherwise) that make or give the impression that TAs are directly accountable for pupil outcomes. As Jane Friswell, the CEO of Nasen, puts it: 'The Code's key message is ultimately that every teacher is responsible and accountable for all pupils in their class, *wherever or whoever* the pupils are working with' (Friswell 2013, emphasis added).

So, the Code of Practice makes the teacher's role clear, but the TA's role remains somewhat vague.

Government policy: no plans and no power

A major external influence on school-level decision-making is government policy. School leaders and teachers have been used to turbulence in recent years. A plethora of new policies have been introduced (often at whirlwind pace) and many existing ones have been scrapped or extensively modified. Yet when it comes to policy directly affecting TAs (who, remember, account for 25 per cent of the school workforce), things have been much quieter.

At the time of writing, the government's position on TAs is relatively clear. The worrying media headlines in response to the Reform report mentioned in Chapter 1 prompted a debate in the House of Commons on 18 March 2014 entitled, 'The value of teaching assistants'. Responding to concerns that TA jobs might be under threat, the-then junior education minister, Elizabeth Truss MP, assured the House that 'neither the Department of Education nor the government have any plans or powers to make that [mass redundancies] happen' (Hansard 2014). Decisions relating to the employment and deployment of TAs were, she said, a matter for school leaders, not Whitehall. This message about the government's 'hands-off' approach was reinforced in September 2014 by the education secretary, Nicky Morgan MP (DfE 2014).

'What do Ofsted inspectors want to see?'

Over the last few years, we have given dozens of talks and presentations on our research to school leaders keen to know about the practical implications of our findings. One of the most common questions we get asked in relation to effective TA practice is: 'What do Ofsted inspectors want to see?' We have generally found this is a difficult question to answer, not least because we have had nothing more to inform our view than the Ofsted inspection frameworks and guidance available to schools.

Consistent with the prevailing pedagogical trend in the English education system of giving primacy to the transfer of knowledge from subject experts, we would expect the School Inspection Handbook to have much more to say about the role of teachers than TAs – and indeed it does (Ofsted, 2015).[1] Yet coverage in relation to TAs is exceptionally scant, perhaps reflecting the government's non-interventionist approach to their deployment. Much like the Code of Practice, the teacher's role is sharpened and clarified, but the TA's role is, by comparison, indistinct.

We think school leaders should use the openness in the Ofsted guidance to their advantage. Because the use and contribution of TAs are terms that are not further defined by Ofsted – in other words, there are no specific expectations in relation to what inspectors are looking for – school leaders can occupy this space, giving the role legitimate and operational definition.

Framing change: summary

So where does this leave us? We know the widespread models of using TAs are ineffective, and that you, as a school leader, have the power and freedom to innovate. It is your responsibility to define the use of and contribution made by TAs in your school, and provide the evidence that your decisions about this have positive outcomes – the measures of which you can also define. It is your overarching responsibility to ensure teachers are responsible for the progress and development of pupils with SEN. Teachers themselves will need to take ownership of this, as they are accountable for pupil outcomes.

This clarification and shoring up of roles and responsibilities concerning teaching and learning at the school level and classroom level opens up a space in which we can begin to imagine distinct and alternative, but complementary, roles for TAs.

Asserting values

It is important to note that simply correcting for the ineffective use of TAs and ineffective TA practice is not going to be enough to bring about the truly transformative change we think is possible in every school. For example, encouraging teachers to plan a role for TAs in lessons is essential, but there must be some kind of effective feedback mechanism too. In Chapter 6, we show how to achieve this. Similarly, we cannot just ask TAs not to spoon-feed answers to children; we must ensure their talk to pupils is more meaningful. We address this in Chapter 5.

Put simply, we need to build a positive alternative to how we use TAs in schools, which must be underpinned by a clear vision set by the senior leadership team (SLT), who then take decisions and drive action consistent with it. While some headteachers might prefer we staked out the territory in which to think and act in relation to school inspection, to do so would be to suggest that school leaders should determine strategic decision-making only in relation to extrinsic forces.

This can lead to some rather perverse behaviour. We have heard a number of stories of how schools and teachers prepare for inspection. Teachers pull out all the stops – meeting with TAs before lessons; producing detailed lesson plans clearly indicating the TA's role; and differentiating for every pupil in the class – only for everything to revert back to normal (no meeting; no lesson plan; fewer levels of differentiation, if any) when the inspection team has left. Such behaviour is concerning and typical of what happens when the driving force for change is compliance with a perception of what Ofsted expects to see, and which anyway is a mirage. We are of the view that the drive to establishing effective school-wide TA practice represented by the MITA process, and the outcomes it can produce, *is* what Ofsted would like to see.

Setting your whole-school vision for TAs should prompt you to think like a leader, not like a senior inspector. Moreover, this part of the process allows you to assert intrinsically positive values, such as equality and fairness, to ensure the implicit forms of educational inequality and the double standards that TA support has inadvertently come to represent (Giangreco 2003; Giangreco et al. 2005; Webster et al. 2010) are reversed.

Your MITA team: 'a guiding coalition'

Kotter's second step for bringing about change requires the creation of a guiding coalition. This group must possess the authority and power to lead change and take top-level decisions. As it happens, schools already have in place such a body of people in the shape of the SLT, and it is their job to define the vision for the TA workforce – perhaps with some input from the governing body.

In the initial stages of implementing the MITA process, we recommend you schedule time to have open and unrestrained debates about the role of TAs in your school, and to begin fleshing out your vision. Having this dedicated time is essential. School leaders that participate in the MITA programme value the time away from school it provides, as it gives them time and space to think and discuss without interruptions.

As in the MITA programme, you too will need to assemble your 'MITA team'. It may not be practical or desirable to include all members of SLT in your team, especially if it is particularly numerous. However, it must include and be led by the headteacher or principal.

More broadly, you should be looking to bring together a coalition of willing and likeminded colleagues. As we mentioned in the Introduction, you need to recruit members of staff willing to support your vision and to contribute to developing and testing strategies on the ground. Membership of your team could extend to teachers and TAs, but keep your MITA team to a manageable size. This helps ensure your initial trials are manageable too, and will not overburden staff.

We suggest you have protected time for regular team meetings to discuss progress. Set dates for meetings months in advance – and stick to them! It is tempting and often too easy to 'bump' such meetings to attend to other matters. But remember: these are behaviours consistent with stewardship, not leadership.

You will require honesty and candour from your team, but people in less senior positions may feel intimidated about speaking truth to power. Therefore, consider drawing up some protocols at your first meeting about how discussions will be conducted in order to protect participants and encourage an open and productive dialogue.

Developing a clear shared vision

Having set the context for the discussions, you need develop a clear vision for your school. This is the third step on Kotter's model. It is useful to adopt the approach of starting with the end in mind; that is, defining the point you want to reach. Constantly referring back to this goal will inform and drive the developmental work on the ground.

To help you, we suggest you and your SLT discuss and begin formulating responses to the following question:

> What do you want the role, purpose and contribution of TAs to be in your school?

Let us clarify our terms. *Role* relates to the part(s) played by a TA in a particular situation; this may lead you to create 'types' of TA role. The reason why these roles are needed is the *purpose*: put the needs of all the pupils in your school at the heart of change. Finally, your decisions should lead to a direct or indirect impact on learning; in other words, there is an identifiable *contribution* made by TAs. We will build on this in the next chapter on TA deployment.

One key thing to consider in your exploration of this question is to clarify how your staff use the term 'support' and what they understand it to mean. When school leaders, SENCos, teachers and TAs are asked the question, 'what do TAs do?', the responses are very often couched in terms of 'providing support': for teachers; for pupils with SEN; in the classroom; with teaching; with learning. The trouble is that even with further questioning, all of these notions of support are fuzzy and tell us very little about what TAs actually do and how it impacts on learning.

Your aim is to identify a clear vision to articulate what you want TAs to do in your school to enhance teaching and learning, and improve pupil outcomes; in other words, pin down specific definitions of support. These should be limited to no more than three or four types of support; anything over this number and the fuzziness is likely to return.

It is essential you do not limit the discussion or thinking to the current ways of doing things, or to what you only *think* is possible under current, and perhaps, restricted conditions. Avoid the temptation to focus on 'outliers'; that is, how to overcome specific circumstances or attitudes that may threaten the realisation of your vision. In short, this discussion is the time to set aside any limitations and imagine a whole new way of doing things. The material in the rest of this book can inform contributions to this discussion. Chapters 4 and 5 on TAs' deployment and practice are particularly relevant to generating ideas.

The bigger picture

Your vision for your TA workforce is likely to link or overlap with other areas of school improvement; for example, managing teachers' workload and closing the attainment gap between disadvantaged pupils and their peers. Making such connections is to be encouraged, as it reminds us that schools are 'ecosystems'.

As we have already mentioned, the work of the Education Endowment Foundation and others is useful in terms of helping schools to make informed decisions about interventions to raise attainment. But there is a danger interventions (and sometimes the issues they are designed to address) are considered in relative isolation, as if apart from the ecosystem in which they sit. Tweaking or introducing a new initiative in one part of the system (e.g. a new TA-led catch-up reading scheme) can have implications or opportunity costs elsewhere, for which we must account (e.g. missed curriculum coverage; disjuncture between approaches to the teaching of reading that may confuse learners).

TAs are a big part of the current and lively conversation on effective, evidence-informed interventions. In the following chapters, we provide detail on the practical 'real world' strategies that can help you to realise your vision. But as we proceed, we inevitably narrow the discourse somewhat by focusing only on TAs and not, for example, SEN provision more broadly. We risk, therefore, atomising problems and solutions, and we could lose sight of how they relate to one another; all of which has hints of stewardship. Hereon in, you need to be mindful of how, as a leader, the various ideas and strategies presented serve not only your vision for TAs, but for your vision for your teachers, your pupils and your school.

Developing an action plan

Schools are complex and dynamic environments in which to successfully implement change on the scale outlined in this book. We would be the first to admit this can be like trying to hit a moving target, so it is useful to consider Timothy Knoster's (Knoster et al. 2000) advice about understanding the essential components of systemic organisational reform. His model of managing complex change suggests that when the components of vision, consensus, skills, incentives, resources and an action plan are all in place, achieving the desired change is far more likely. However, if any one of the five components is missing, the change process is liable to incur problems. For example, without a vision, there is confusion; without resources, there is frustration. And without an action plan, schools are likely to remain 'on the treadmill'. In the absence of a clearly defined path towards the vision, they just keep going over the same old ground.

As you work through the chapters of this book, we recommend you and your SLT begin to draft an action plan. You may have a preferred method or template you use for planning, but for school leaders in need of a starting point, we provide a copy of the action plan template we use on our MITA course in Appendix 2. You can also download an editable version from our website.

You will notice our action plan has three sections relating to deployment, practice and preparedness to help guide your thinking and decision-making. Within each of these headings, we encourage you to consider the actions you need to take that relate: (i) directly to TAs; and (ii) to any teacher-level or school-level action that may also be required. For example, you may decide to deploy TAs in ways that free teachers up to work with pupils with SEN. But if the impact of this action is to be fully realised, you need to ensure your teachers receive specific up-to-date training on how to teach these pupils to maximum effect.

Leading successful change in your school

Having developed your vision and planned the strategies for achieving it, you must use every possible means and opportunity to regularly communicate the vision and strategies. This is the fourth step on Kotter's path to implementing successful change. Schools in the EDTA project and those undertaking the MITA programme use their guiding coalitions to test and model new strategies. These groups are supported in their actions by senior leaders who empower their staff to challenge existing ways of doing things and to take risks. Removing obstacles that could undermine change is important. Your staff should not be held back by thinking that leads them to test 'safe' strategies with a high chance of success. To empower people to act (Kotter's fifth step), you must stress that the outcomes of developmental work – that is, whether a trial worked – have equal value. It is as important to know what does not work and why, as much as it is to know what works successfully and the conditions for success.

Your group of teachers and TAs that pilot strategies should be encouraged to share their learning with colleagues. Kotter refers to 'generating short-term wins' (step 6) that build school-wide support for change. That ideas are generated and shared organically through a peer-led process avoids a sense of top-down imposition and is likely to encourage the participation of more resistant colleagues. Consolidating gains and producing more change (step 7) not only embeds ideas and encourages new ones, but also helps transform the culture of the school. This is essential for institutionalising a positive 'change culture' (step 8), which ensures staff have the right dispositions needed to engage with the continuous drive to school improvement.

Note

1 At the time of writing (summer 2015), the draft of the School Inspection Handbook was awaiting minor revisions, ahead of its implementation at the start of the 2015/16 school year.

Chapter 4

The deployment of TAs

Introduction

The DISS project findings made clear that aspects of TA deployment need to be challenged and changed in order to avoid the unintentionally damaging effects their support can have on pupils' academic progress. Decisions about TA deployment are the starting point from which all other decisions about TAs flow.

This is the premise of the key deployment question for school leaders we set out in the previous chapter, in terms of defining TAs' role, purpose and contribution. In this chapter, we provide some additional framing and set out ideas to help explore this question in depth. While this book is directed principally at school leaders, you may be reading this book as a teacher or trainee teacher working in a school that (as far as you know) is not considering such a process of restructuring (in which case, you might want to anonymously leave a copy of this book in your headteacher's pigeonhole!). There are, of course, things teachers can do irrespective of wider school action, and we have flagged these ideas throughout the rest of this book in sections headed 'Teacher-level decisions'.

Reviewing and defining the role of the TA: school-level decisions

The findings from the DISS project prompt a fundamental question school leaders *must* address: given that we found TAs have an ineffective instructional role in classrooms, should they have a pedagogical role at all? Should they teach pupils directly?

If the answer is yes – and most schools we have worked with have taken this route – we need to work out what this pedagogical role should be. If, on the other hand, we take the view TAs should not have a pedagogical role, then we must again decide what this non-pedagogical role should be. In our view, this issue has been given far too little attention, even though it is at the heart of many other issues connected to the use of TAs. Both views are defensible, but both require careful consideration of the consequences. Throughout this chapter, we raise some important questions you will need to consider when assigning broadly pedagogical and non-pedagogical roles to TAs.

The process of review and redefinition of TAs' roles across the school must be initiated by the SLT, but it is essential teachers and TAs are involved in the early deliberations and piloting of alternative methods.

The audit process set out in Chapter 2 allows you to review the present deployment of TAs in your school, and it will reveal the extent to which your TAs teach pupils, both in and away from the classroom. It will also identify the non-pedagogical roles they have (e.g. doing administrative tasks for teachers). Schools that have surveyed staff about their perceptions of the TA role have found the results of this process very revealing; in some cases, a wide and unexpected variation in perceptions was found. The findings from staff consultations can be used to inform decisions about formally defining TA roles across the school.

It may be thought best to combine elements of a pedagogical and a non-pedagogical role for some or all of your TAs. This will be informed by what you find in your audit of TAs' individual strengths and skills sets; some TAs will be more appropriately deployed in teaching roles than others if, for example, their subject knowledge is particularly strong. This would be a school-level choice, setting the boundaries for classroom-level deployment decisions made by individual teachers.

Non-pedagogical and pedagogical roles for TAs

We will now explore the various options and decisions that arise from your decisions to deploy TAs in non-pedagogical and pedagogical roles. We will explore each in turn in more detail, following some guidance on deciding your staffing structure. Before we do, however, it is worth setting out briefly what we mean by non-pedagogical and pedagogical TA roles.

A non-pedagogical role for TAs

If you choose to replace TAs' direct teaching role with a non-teaching role, you will need to define their new role and identify the tasks you feel contribute to the overall effectiveness of the school. The research evidence suggests three main non-pedagogical roles TAs can adopt (see Blatchford et al. 2012b):

1   Supporting the teacher in terms of carrying out routine tasks, such as preparing and organising materials.
2   Helping with classroom organisation and ensuring lessons run more smoothly by encouraging pupils to focus on tasks and 'nipping in the bud' any off-task or disruptive behaviour.
3   Providing direct support for pupils with physical/mobility or emotional needs.

In this section, we additionally flag the potential for TAs to take on a parent liaison role. The importance and value of such a role, acting as a trusted mediator between school and home, is gaining prominence as greater emphasis is placed on parental engagement in pupils' learning and school life in general.

As a school leader, you must give thought to the optimum balance of direct and indirect forms of TA support for pupils and teachers (e.g. performing tasks that require and do not require a high degree of instructional interaction with pupils) and the possibility of developing a select variety of TA roles. We return to this point later.

If you decide to limit the role of some or all of your TAs to non-pedagogical roles, the implementation will expose the need for changes in TAs' preparation and training for these newly configured roles. Day-to-day preparation for their work will also become a clearer issue and steps will be needed to make this effective (see Chapter 6).

A pedagogical role for TAs

The audit process will reveal the extent and form of TAs' pedagogical role. As we saw with the DISS project findings, it is likely that TAs in your school have a considerable teaching role, which may be more substantive than you initially imagined.

The complete picture provided by the audit will raise questions about the TAs' role both alongside teachers in classrooms and away from classrooms and teachers. The DISS project findings challenge you to review the present deployment of TAs in a pedagogical role in these two contexts and to make changes where required.

If you choose to retain a role for TAs in which they have an instructional role with pupils, you need to define and agree the details of what this should involve, and express it formally in the shape of a school policy on TA deployment. The policy encapsulates and expands on your vision. In the DISS project, it was evident that the leadership decisions that would have achieved the coordination and consistency across the school often had not been taken. In the absence of a vision or policy, the situation on the ground was often *ad hoc* and subject to enormous variation across classes, as individual teachers had been left to make the deployment decisions. We will return to the content of a school policy below.

Some important questions to ask about the pedagogical role of TAs

- Is it reasonable to expect TAs to be *as effective as* teachers when teaching pupils, given they do not have the same levels of training?
- Where is the appropriate boundary between the teaching roles of teachers and TAs?
- What is the limit, in terms of responsibility and accountability to parents and the school governing body, of TAs who teach?
- What does 'working under the supervision of the teacher' actually mean and look like in your school?
- Should teachers delegate the teaching of pupils with the most demanding learning needs to TAs, who generally do not possess the relevant teaching qualifications?
- Are TAs who teach given the status, professional development opportunities, participation in decision-making about teaching and learning, and salaries that reflect these responsibilities?

These are the 'hard' questions that must be addressed when opting to deploy TAs in a pedagogical role. The DISS project showed such questions had not been addressed at the school level, resulting in many forms of ineffective practice and damage being done to pupils' progress, in particular those who were most disadvantaged. In many schools, this situation prevails. Individual teachers are left to make their own deployment decisions, perhaps interpreting their perceived view of what someone else believes constitutes appropriate use of TAs – be that SLT, the SENCo, Ofsted or parents of pupils with SEN. Teachers take these decisions having had little or no training or guidance to inform them, and they have seldom been asked to justify their choices or evaluate the effectiveness of their decisions.

The process leading to clearly defined pedagogical roles needs to include teachers, TAs and SLT. It will need to start from a fully informed position via the audit, and the issue of the appropriate level for particular deployment choices across the school and within classrooms will have to be addressed. Answering this question will clarify what your school policy will need to cover in detail and will provide a framework within which individual teachers can operate, making it clearer which decisions are permissible when deploying TAs to teach pupils, in or out of the classroom.

Drawing up a school policy

Teachers and TAs will need to have clear guidelines to help them conform to the redefined TA roles. The best way to provide such guidance is to develop a school policy on TA deployment. We recommend you begin drafting your policy alongside the decision-making process set out in this book. You may already have some ideas worth capturing, and these will be shaped and clarified by the discussions you have and the things you pilot in classrooms. The process of the policy's development and its implementation will establish a shared understanding of the boundaries between the roles of teachers and TAs, in terms of how the TAs can be managed by teachers to maximum benefit.

Pupils will also need to be made aware of the ways in which the school will deploy TAs, since many may have become dependent on them. All teachers will need to explain to their pupils the new forms of teamwork they have agreed to introduce in their classes and which require deploying TAs in ways that depart from previous practice.

The parents of pupils with Statements of SEN or EHCPs should also be included in this information sharing exercise. The benefits of new, modified or different models of TA deployment will need to be explained to parents who have become familiar with – or expect – particular models of TA usage. You might find educational psychologists helpful in mediating this process (see Webster 2014a).

Such major changes will present challenges to everyone within the school. They will not be fully operational immediately and there are bound to be periods of adjustment along the way as new forms of practice become embedded. The more thorough and open the processes of consultation, data collection, decision-making, dissemination and implementation, the smoother the road to more effective ways of deploying your TAs will be.

Naturally, the needs of your school are different to other schools, so it will be essential for you to write a policy that reflects the vision for your school line by line. You may decide that rather than write a separate policy, you will expand and integrate the necessary content relating to TAs into your teaching and learning policy. Either way, it is helpful to have some sense of what that content might look like. We have produced an editable TA policy template that you can download from our website: www.maximsingtas.co.uk. It specifies the areas we believe your policy should cover, using the components of the WPR model as a structure, and some suggestions to consider. However, the development of your policy should not be treated as a 'cut and paste' exercise using this draft. Make sure you 'own' the content.

Your policy should be a 'living document', embodying what you do in relation to the employment and deployment of your TA workforce, but it does not need to run to pages and pages. Some schools have found it helpful to distill their policy into a one-page summary. One way of doing this is in terms of an agreement setting out what TAs can expect from SLT, what TAs can expect from teachers, and what the SLT and teachers can expect from TAs. An example of such an agreement can be found in Appendix 3 and also on our website.

Key recommendations on thinking through a pedagogical role for TAs

- Recognise the importance of clarifying the pedagogical role of TAs, relative to teachers.
- With your SLT, address the hard questions suggested above and use the answers to frame your philosophy about TA deployment.
- Draft a policy on TA deployment, setting out a framework within which teachers will have some flexibility at the classroom level. Be clear about how teachers will be able to deploy TAs and what is no longer permissible.
- Be flexible. Modify your draft policy as you work through the MITA process to reflect what you learn about what works and what does not work.

Clarifying the role of each TA

Decisions about staffing structure

Many schools have been prompted to participate in our MITA programme at the UCL Institute of Education by a need to overhaul their staffing structure. We have worked with a number of headteachers who were relatively new to post and who had inherited a workforce containing a high number of TAs, mainly on part-time contracts, each with idiosyncratic hours of work. This situation had been created over time by a long-serving predecessor. For some schools, there was a clear need to consider and clarify the appropriate role of each TA in their school. For others, there was an added need to reduce the overall number of TAs they employed, moving to fewer TAs working more (typically full-time) hours.

School leaders are increasingly being moved to take more deliberate and conscious decisions regarding the deployment of TAs, moving away from the routine default position of deploying all TAs on the same basis in a generic role, to a more purposeful and methodical alignment of specific roles and individuals. A sense that the TA role deserves some form of professional status or recognition tends to accompany the view among school leaders that 'something must be done' about the current situation.

It is essential you base your decisions about your staffing structure on a careful analysis of the needs of all the pupils in your school. As we have already made clear, when it comes to ensuring the best learning outcomes for the most vulnerable pupils, your first line of defence is high-quality teaching, planned for and delivered by teachers. The starting point for thinking about remodelling the role of TAs does not start with TAs and their support at all, but teachers and teaching.

Defining the needs of the pupils in your school

The needs of your pupils will be many and varied, but you and your SLT will be able to make a broad list of needs that should apply to virtually every pupil in your school. Focus this list on areas related to learning or approaches to learning. Your list might include, but not be limited to, the ways all pupils need to acquire:

- a secure foundation in reading, writing, spelling, language and numeracy
- knowledge and competence across a broad range of curriculum subjects
- attentiveness and listening skills
- an enquiring mind
- a sense of entitlement to, and appetite for, knowledge and self-improvement
- metacognitive skills (i.e. knowing how to know, or learning how to learn)
- information handling skills (e.g. how to evaluate evidence)
- confidence in the face of challenges
- mental toughness to cope with uncertainty
- strength to accept failure as part of learning
- independent working skills and self-reliance
- an understanding and acceptance of boundaries
- skills to interact and collaborate with others
- skills to maintain positive relationships with peers
- skills for honest self-reflection.

There will, of course, be a smaller group of pupils, principally those with SEN, who have particular needs that must be met, but which are not directly related to learning. These needs might include, but not be limited to: physical or sensory impairments; mental health; emotional difficulties; speech and communication. You will need to list these needs too.

Draw a Venn diagram on a large sheet of paper or on a whiteboard. Label one circle, 'Teachers' role and responsibilities', and label the other circle, 'TAs' role and contribution'. Avoid using the word 'responsibility' in relation to TAs, as the language of accountability is not helpful here. Now map the items on your list of pupils' needs that are clearly within the teachers' sphere of responsibility onto the teacher circle of your diagram. Debate the items on the list that are left over and place them on the diagram. Can you agree and clarify a boundary around the teachers' role and responsibilities? What space opens up around the TA role, and what sort of contribution might they be able to make to meet the needs of pupils?

Look for the ways TAs can 'add value' to what teachers do. A useful exercise to try with your teaching staff is to ask them to envisage the classroom as it would be *without* a TA. How will they organise things in order to provide the best educational experience for *all* pupils in the class (e.g. via high quality teaching), including those typically supported by a TA? Following this, think about how the additional resource – the TA – can be reintroduced to the classroom. What can they do to help teaching and learning, and/or to help keep the classroom running efficiently and effectively – *without* replacing the teacher?

We have found that a number of schools get stuck on the idea that a role must be found for every TA (and some teachers) employed by the school. But this positions adults as the focus of decision-making, rather than the pupils. As a result of undertaking the kind of exercises we described above, some schools have found that in order to avoid compromising on the input required to fully meet their pupils' needs, they have had to expand their teaching workforce and shrink their TA workforce. Uncomfortable though it is to state, it is naive not to acknowledge that the process of rethinking your staffing structure *on the basis of a clear analysis of pupils' needs* may result in some staff having their hours of work reduced or roles becoming surplus to need.

Of course, there is a place for considering the needs of adults too – specifically your teachers. TAs will be needed to ensure your teachers are freed up to deliver high-quality teaching, for instance. Below we address specific points to consider when assigning non-pedagogical and pedagogical roles to individual TAs, and how they can be used in direct and indirect ways to ensure the needs of pupils are met. But first, we set out the two main ways in which you and your SLT can approach decisions about determining your staffing structure.

Case study

Clarifying the role and purpose of TAs

The staff audit at one special school revealed that teachers felt TAs tended to take on too much responsibly for completing tasks, and that this affected the development of pupils' ability to work independently. The SLT conducted learning walks and observed that TAs were often passive in class and their feedback to pupils on learning was unfocused and vague. Ofsted inspectors had also commented on the inconsistency in practice and how not all TAs were proactive.

Knowing that the potential existed within their large TA workforce (they had 61 TAs and 14 teachers), the SLT set out to move away from the 'care' role that TAs had adopted to a role that would better support learning, and to make this consistent across the school. The SLT introduced a programme to reposition the TA role, encouraging thought and discussion about the purpose of learning and school in the lives of pupils. Training was put in place to help TAs interact with pupils in ways that supported learning goals more purposefully.

Further learning walks to assess progress revealed that TAs' interactions were more focused on learning and less vague than previously found. The programme had been added to the induction package for new staff.

The blank page approach

The first approach is what we might call the 'blank page' approach. This method assumes you are starting from scratch, as if you do not have any TAs in your school. As we set out in the previous chapter on defining your vision, as a headteacher, you have the freedom to determine everything about the composition and nature of your TA workforce. You can decide the TA staffing structure you want in terms of the broad roles you require in order to meet the needs of your pupils. Questions you need to ask include:

- How many TAs do you want to have a predominantly pedagogical role, and how will they be assigned (e.g. to classes, subjects and/or year groups; to interventions programmes)?
- Do you require TAs to provide lesson cover for teachers? If so, how many?
- How many 'classroom helpers' do you need (e.g. TAs with a non-pedagogical role who can assist teachers with routine tasks in the classroom)?

- How many TAs are needed to support pupils with physical/mobility needs?
- How many TAs do you require in a nurturing capacity (e.g. Emotional Literacy Support Assistants)?

Here, we couch the questions in terms of the personnel required, which can assume these TA roles are full-time posts. Of course, there are other ways in which these questions can be presented; for example, in terms of how many hours of TA time are required to cover planning, preparation and assessment (PPA) time for teachers. However, we note there may be implications for pay if, for example, you deploy an HLTA as a classroom helper for part of the week; the use of 'split contracts' (paying TAs at different rates depending on the tasks they do) is not in line with the principles of the National Agreement that initiated this practice (WAMG 2008).

Some schools we know have found it helpful to use national standards for obtaining HLTA status and TA role profiles provided by their local authority, which outline the key 'responsibilities' and entry-level requirements for TAs at several graded levels, to help make decisions about staffing. Using the blank page approach, you will be able to establish a broad set of TA roles, which are distinct from one another and from the role of teachers.

The next step is to map your existing TAs on to the roles you identified in the exercise above, using the evidence from your audit of TAs' skills and qualifications. Some TAs have strengths in providing warmth, empathy and encouragement, and have a firm but sensitive authority, which would make them suited to working with pupils in nurturing roles. Other TAs may have a degree in a particular subject specialism and would be suitably deployed to support lessons in that subject.

The key principle is to develop roles more consciously and purposefully, and to ensure and specify the minimum level of expertise expected for each role. Every effort must be made to avoid defaulting to the current and widespread – not to mention ineffective – forms of TA deployment, which do not vary across year groups, classes, subjects or the individuals who occupy these roles.

There may be roles that are not filled by individuals, and, conversely, TAs who do not have roles within your new structure. However, this process will highlight training needs for specific individuals, who can be trained to meet the role requirements.

The retrofit approach

We call the second approach to deciding your TA staffing structure the 'retrofit' approach, meaning that the process described above is essentially reversed. You begin the retrofit approach by examining the results of your TA skills audit, and then base your staffing structure on these results. It is important to note this approach will not necessarily give your school the TA staffing structure you *need* or that aligns with an ideal model; in other words, it is less consistent with centering your approach on putting the needs of pupils first.

The retrofit approach involves first confirming the levels at which your TAs are working. Again, some schools have used the aforementioned TA role profiles or similar frameworks, as it helps ascertain the degree to which TAs are working within their current grading. It can also reveal whether TAs are being deployed to their maximum effect or whether there are any TAs who are being stretched (perhaps unfairly) beyond their current capabilities and level of training.

Once you feel you know your TAs well enough, you can select the criteria on which you will base their position within your new structure. Their qualifications, specialisms, strengths, experience of particular year groups, subjects and partnerships with teachers, may all figure in your decisions. As with the blank page method, training needs will be readily identifiable via this approach.

Case study

Using audit data to inform TA deployment

The SLT wanted to know more about how TAs spent their time, so they conducted a mini research project. TAs were asked to complete a systematic timelog each day for a week, logging what they did every five minutes. Classroom observations were also conducted. The findings were consistent with the results from the DISS project, revealing a 'Velcro TA' effect for pupils with Statements of SEN.

On the basis of their findings, the SLT set out to redistribute TAs' time; from spending 80 per cent of their time in class and 20 per cent delivering curriculum interventions, to spending 50 per cent of their time in class, 30 per cent delivering interventions, and 20 per cent preparing resources (on which they had training). The changes were designed to ensure that teachers took on more responsibility for working with pupils with SEN, for which they too received training.

Consultation

Changing your TA staffing structure may involve wider consultations as inevitable modifications to contracts and conditions of employment have legal ramifications. Many local authorities have a policy and/or adviser on staff restructuring to whom leaders of maintained schools could refer. Schools falling outside local authority control may have to consult their own advisers on employment law. It may also be necessary to consult with local union representatives (e.g. Unison).

At the school level, school leaders may not be able to implement changes without approval from the governing body. Governors are often consulted on developments that have financial implications for the school. On this issue, it is worth noting that restructuring your TA workforce may incur some short-term costs (which would be offset by long-term gains), but we know of no legal bar to undertaking this work.

Key recommendations on clarifying the role of each TA

- Conduct a survey of TAs' skills, qualifications and training received as part of your school audit.
- Review current TA roles and consider having a variety of distinct roles within a new TA staffing structure; for example: direct pupil support roles (including

interventions); classroom support roles; subject-specific roles; and nurturing and pastoral roles.

• Conduct appropriate consultations with legal and union representatives, and the school's governing body.

Defining types of non-pedagogical role for TAs

The overtly non-pedagogical roles TAs can have are broadly concerned with assisting teachers with routine tasks and classroom behaviour, and having a nurturing or welfare role supporting pupils' physical and emotional needs. Here, we also consider a role in relation to parent liaison.

Supporting the work of teachers: administrative support

Perhaps the most extreme expression of a non-pedagogical role is one that requires little, if any, interaction with pupils, and instead helps teachers with their routine clerical tasks (photocopying, etc.). We know from the DISS project such deployment of TAs and other support staff contributed to reducing teacher workloads and positively affected their levels of stress and job satisfaction (Blatchford et al. 2012b). When TAs take on teachers' routine admin tasks, it frees up time for teachers to focus on teaching tasks, such as lesson planning or assessment. This, in turn, improves their teaching. We refer to this form of TA support as having an *indirect* impact on pupils: TAs help teachers to help pupils.

We doubt many school leaders would be convinced that this model will be appropriate for their entire current TA workforce, but there may be a case for developing, say, one TA post for this type of work. If so, you will need to identify the tasks that define this role.

Teacher-level decisions

Teachers deploying TAs to take on their routine tasks will need to define which tasks they want them to perform; there may be some that individual teachers wish to retain, such as classroom display (we found this to be the case in the DISS project). The tasks may, to some extent, have a degree of regularity and pattern to them, but they will also inevitably have an element of variety, reflecting the work of the pupils and teachers across the school year.

Supporting the work of teachers: classroom management

The DISS project showed that one way TAs had benefits for teachers was in terms of classroom management. This is another expression of the *indirect* support provided by TAs and appreciated by teachers. Ofsted has, for a long time, pointed out the main behaviour problem in schools is the 'persistent, low-level disruption of lessons that wears down staff and disrupts learning' (2005). The DISS project found the presence of a TA limits the need for teachers to manage this kind of problem. You might consider developing an effective non-instructional role for TAs in which they act as an extra set of eyes and ears, noticing negative and off-task behaviour, and stepping in to address it without disrupting the teacher's delivery or the flow of the lesson.

We note, however, that while Giangreco and Broer (2005) found TAs spent one-fifth of their time providing behavioural support to pupils, they were relatively untrained and underprepared in this area, and often lacked confidence when it came to managing challenging behaviour. If you develop such roles for TAs, it is imperative those who occupy these positions are thoroughly trained in classroom management techniques and are recognised by staff and pupils as legitimate enforcers of the school's behaviour policy. Teachers, however, must have ultimate responsibility for the management of behaviour in the classroom; it is not a duty to be wholly delegated to TAs.

The limits of this role must be made clear to teachers in order to inform their classroom deployment decisions. They must be aware of what TAs can be expected and not expected to do in these roles. The appropriate use of TAs as classroom behaviour monitors should be covered in your school policy on TAs.

Teacher-level decisions

Low-level disruption can be greatly reduced when TAs are deployed to manage off-task behaviour and ensure pupils are focused, attentive and on-task. This gives teachers more time to teach, thus benefiting everyone in the class.

Teachers must remain in control of motivating pupils, gaining and maintaining their focus, and be responsible for behaviour management overall (and especially for serious incidents). However, there are ways in which the TA can watch for those small signs of negative and off-task behaviour, and step in to address it without disrupting the lesson.

This form of TA deployment will need to be both sensitive and responsive to the emerging needs of the pupils across any particular lesson. TAs are used to sitting as part of the class audience and can pick up on things teachers do not always notice, because they are focused on teaching.

This form of support may be unnecessary if low-level disruption is not an issue in every class, or if some teachers prefer to deal with it themselves. Therefore, the nature and limits of this behaviour monitoring role need to be made explicit to each TA in each teaching and learning context; this may differ between year groups or teaching sets.

Teachers should agree the appropriate forms of intervention with the TA(s) in their class. In the most effective instances we have seen, TAs are able to discreetly capture the attention of disruptive or off-task pupils, and with a look, a gesture or a whisper, quell the disquiet. We have seen many examples of TAs dampen potentially volatile situations, refocus off-task pupils, break up chatter, confiscate sweets, move pupils to other seats and even send them from the room. This limits the distracting effects of individual pupils, and generally keeps the classroom ticking over, allowing the teacher to teach and pupils to learn. Teachers must decide the limits of what TAs will be allowed to do; for example, they may be happy for them to move a pupil to another desk, but not to send them from the classroom.

Teachers may wish to include the TA in the sanctions and rewards policy they use for their class (which should, of course, be in line with whole-school strategies), but ensure there is consistency; pupils are quick to pick up on variations in punishments for the same misdemeanour.

While teachers have the ultimate responsibility for the management of behaviour in the classroom, the pupils will need to know the TA is acting as the teacher's enforcer. It will need to be clear to pupils that teachers have given TAs the power to deal with low-level disruption and that TAs are to be respected and obeyed in this capacity. Teachers must demonstrate they and the TA are a team and that teachers back TAs' judgements. In the worst cases we have seen and had described to us, pupils undermine both the teacher, and particularly the TA, when they divide and rule, playing the teacher's seniority off against the TA's relatively weaker position.

Teachers and TAs must present themselves as a united force. This, together with coaching and mentoring support from teachers, and underpinned by a consistent approach to reprimand and rewards, is what really gives TAs confidence.

Supporting pupils' physical and emotional needs

Some TAs in some schools will already have a role connected to the support of pupils with physical needs of some kind (e.g. mobility, visual or hearing impairment). We also consider such support to have an *indirect* impact on pupil learning, as it helps pupils to access teaching and learning in a physical and/or dispositional sense.

TAs working in this role require, and will likely have received, special training in, for example, handling and physiotherapy techniques, sign language and using special equipment. Such support from TAs is vital for those pupils who might otherwise have to attend a special school, not because of a learning need (some will not have any such difficulties), but because of the accessibility of buildings, equipment and the curriculum.

The issue for school leaders to consider is this: what proportion of the time do TAs in such roles *actually* spend supporting pupils' physical needs, and what proportion of the time do they do other things. While there is clear value in TAs performing roles many teachers will not be able to do concurrent with leading the class (e.g. signing for hearing impaired pupils), the DISS project revealed the problems that occur when TAs with such responsibilities stray into, or are expected to take on, pedagogical functions for which they are far less prepared.

While we do not understate the need for necessary forms of physical support, our research has raised concerns about the assumptions teachers of mainstream classes make about the need for, and level of, support they should provide for pupils with physical needs. Although it is true not all pupils with physical needs have learning needs, many do. And although TAs who support such pupils have often had specialist training to assist physical needs, it should not be assumed they have had quality training to support their learning needs as well (Anderson and Finney 2008; Lamb 2009; Norwich and Lewis 2001). Michael Giangreco (2003) refers to this as the 'training trap': the tendency for teachers to relinquish instruction of pupils with SEN to TAs who have received more or less any kind of training, no matter how scant. We would also add that some school leaders and teachers also fall into the trap when they assume holding an advanced qualification (an A level or degree) in a particular subject indicates anything at all about a TA's ability to teach and to advance learning.

This speaks to issues concerning the preparedness of TAs, which we shall address in Chapter 6. However, the two points to make here are that, as the results from the

Making a Statement (MAST) study very clearly show, when teachers fall into the training trap, it increases the separation between teachers and TA-supported pupils, and pupils can develop an unhelpful dependency on the TA (Webster and Blatchford 2013, 2014).

Your audit will reveal whether there is capacity for TAs in such roles to perform other roles at times when they are not supporting pupils' physical needs. For example, if the supported pupil is able to work independently in a lesson, this creates an opportunity for them to assist the teacher or other pupils in another way (in either a pedagogical or non-pedagogical role). The point here is that if you decide to expand the role of these TAs, it must be clear to them and teachers what the extended limits of their new role are, and new duties must be supported by training.

TAs that support pupils' emotional needs have roles that are particularly well delineated, as they typically have less to do with instruction. These TAs are likely to deliver specific programmes aimed at exploring and developing pupils' emotional literacy and coping skills. This role is a different expression of the paraprofessional role. While it should be the role of other professionals, such as counsellors, to deal with pupils' complex emotional problems, TAs can provide invaluable support to these wider processes by helping pupils to share thoughts and feelings.

Results from the DISS project showed teachers value the knowledge TAs have of pupils because they worked so closely with them and therefore hear about important things in their life that influence their mood and wellbeing. Additionally, TAs often have knowledge about pupils based on the fact they live in the same neighbourhood, unlike teachers, who are more likely to live out of the school's catchment area. Therefore, TAs can be more aware of how family and community life affects pupils.

Fraser and Meadows (2008) found pupils characterised the best TAs as demonstrating care, kindliness, friendliness, helpfulness, warmth and attentiveness. Dunne et al. (2008) highlight TAs' functional priorities in terms of a predominantly nurturing role. Therefore, it is perhaps unsurprising that we have found interactions between TAs and pupils are often less formal and more intimate than those between teachers and pupils; pupils viewed TAs as being closer to 'their level' than teachers.

Many TAs have the background and dispositions well suited to supporting pupils' pastoral needs, and you may choose to develop some specific non-pedagogical roles to capitalise on this. We are aware of a number of schools that train TAs to become Emotional Literacy Support Assistants (ELSAs).[1] TAs qualify following a structured programme of training and supervision from educational psychologists. ELSAs plan and deliver individual and small group support programmes to help pupils with social and emotional difficulties to recognise, understand and manage their emotions, in order to increase their wellbeing and success in school. While such roles are underpinned by training and support, we argue there are particular risks that can stem from TAs selecting, planning, delivering and assessing interventions with little input from teachers, of which you need to be aware. We will deal with this issue in more detail later.

Parent liaison

Parental support and engagement are critical factors in how well children achieve. Schools have long been concerned with the lack of engagement exhibited by some parents in their child's learning. In some cases, this can be explained by parents' own negative experiences of school and learning. Some parents develop a distrust of authority and distance themselves from schools and other social institutions.

Such attitudes are often exaggerated among parents of lower-income families. There are a higher proportion of pupils with SEN from lower-income families compared with those from middle-income and higher-income families. Schools serving families in areas of deprivation often find it more difficult to engage with parents of the pupils who need the most support.

As we have mentioned, a school typically draws its TA workforce from the catchment area it serves. This, together with the personal qualities listed above, puts TAs in a strong position to act as effective mediators or 'connectors' between the school and parents.

We do not intend to provide any further guidance in this book on developing parent liaison or support roles for TAs. If this interests you, you might like to consider a home-liaison role (e.g. along the lines of the local authority portage scheme), a supporting (not a lead) role in structured conversations with parents[2] or family interventions, such as the Positive Parenting Programme.[3] Your local authority will be able to advise you.

Key recommendations on defining the non-pedagogical roles of TAs

- Define the remit of non-pedagogical roles; for example, in terms of the routine tasks TAs should and should not do; or the appropriate level of intervention in managing behaviour.
- When thinking about how TAs can add value to teaching, capitalise on things TAs are well placed to do (e.g. monitor behaviour).
- Look for efficiencies in TA time. Are there other things they could be doing when they are not, for example, supporting pupils' physical needs?
- Ensure pupils are clear about the role of the TA, and that teachers and TAs adopt a team approach.
- Ensure any role change or extension is supported by training and is consistent with school policies (e.g. on behaviour management).

Defining a pedagogical role for TAs

The decision to deploy some or all of your TAs in a pedagogical role (in whole or in part) prompts a set of further issues school leaders need to address. Based on our research, there are particular questions we suggest you ask when defining the composition and parameters of TAs' pedagogical role. We summarise these below before exploring each in turn:

1   What role should TAs have as part of the school's provision for lower-attaining pupils and those with SEN?
2   What is the role of TAs (and teachers) in planning, delivering and assessing intervention programmes?
3   Should TAs lead classes as part of the school's PPA and/or short-term teacher cover arrangements?

4   Should changes be made to the allocation of TAs across classes, year groups and/ or subjects, and how does the school make best use of TAs in these contexts?

5   Are changes needed to TAs' job specifications, conditions of employment and salaries? How will these changes affect TAs already in post and any future appointments?

You may decide some individual TAs should have greater pedagogical responsibilities than others; for example, given the results of your audit of TAs' skills, some might be more appropriately deployed to lead classes as part of PPA arrangements than others. In which case, you will need to ask the questions above with individual TAs in mind to determine the limitations of their pedagogical role. TAs may have particular strengths in specific curriculum areas, but do not assume being qualified to degree level in a particular subject means someone is able to teach or advance learning.

The questions above are useful for determining the outermost limits of the pedagogical role; in other words, just how far should the TAs' teaching role extend into the territory of the teachers' teaching role, given that there should be a distinction between the two? As we noted, our research has revealed many teachers have a view about the encroachment of TAs on their professional teaching role – some are more positive than others (see Blatchford et al. 2012b) – but rarely do they look this issue full in the face and make decisions about how it affects their classroom practice. It is vital, therefore, to set a school-level context for any teacher-level decisions, and in no case is this more important than when considering the provision of pupils with SEN.

TAs and pupils with SEN

The most serious questions raised by the DISS project findings concerned schools' provision for the education of pupils with SEN. As we have explained, the damage done to their progress can be linked to the way TAs are deployed to teach them *in place of* teachers. The MAST study showed that for pupils with the highest level of need (those with Statements), TAs tend to take on the role of their primary educator. School arrangements relying on a high level of TA support have been shown to create a greater separation effect for these pupils, in terms of estrangement from the classroom, the teacher, the mainstream curriculum and peers (Webster and Blatchford 2013).

In both the DISS and EDTA projects, we found a worrying tendency for teachers – particularly those in secondary schools – to assume that planning and meeting the learning needs of pupils with SEN was the responsibility of someone else: often the SENCo or, more vaguely, the Learning Support department. As a school leader, you will need to address this.

Teachers must become the adult with whom pupils with SEN have regular, sustained and focused interactions, and these pupils must remain part of the teaching and learning experience provided in the classroom as much as possible.

Perhaps the clearest message from the DISS project is that TAs must not be routinely deployed to teach lower-attaining pupils and those with SEN. The SEN Code of Practice makes it very clear that such deployment practices are not adequate if schools are to ensure the best possible provision for those who struggle most. It is teachers –

not the SENCo or TAs – who are responsible for the progress and development of pupils. The SENCo should be teachers' first port of call for help and support, but it is not for them (or TAs for that matter) to do their job for them. You should make it clear you will be looking for evidence of teachers taking responsibility for the teaching and learning of *all* pupils as part of your monitoring processes.

Case studies

Using the SEN Code of Practice to inform deployment

The team of 18 TAs in a large secondary school was originally employed to work with 20 pupils with Statements of SEN. This had led to a number of difficulties, including pupils becoming dependent on support from a regular TA and TAs being stretched across too many curriculum areas. Coinciding with the introduction of the 2014 SEN Code of Practice, the school moved to a faculty-based system, where TAs were assigned to a specific curriculum area. As the SLT explained: 'We anticipated that the move was going to be a significant change for both TAs and teachers, but we felt it was the best way forward to overcome the difficulties we were facing'.

Presence vs. impact: provision for pupils with SEN

In their considerations of alternative models of TA deployment (e.g. locating TAs within subject departments), schools in the EDTA project – and in particular, secondary schools – weighed up how they could implement these new models while retaining enough TA hours to meet the support needs of pupils with a Statement for SEN. The need for continuity of support was seen as important for effective provision. TAs, therefore, remained inextricably linked with the provision for SEN, and it seemed that in some cases, parental pressure might have been a driving factor in maintaining the deployment of TAs in this way.

One secondary school found that these parental expectations were heightened during the period of discussing transition from primary to secondary school. Parents of a pupil with a Statement requested that their child received one-to-one support from a TA in secondary school, as he had in primary school. The SENCo, who was acutely aware of the negative impact this form of TA deployment could have on pupil outcomes, wanted to challenge the tendency for parents to expect – and even demand – that their child should have one-to-one TA support in circumstances where teachers could provide more effective input. Achieving this, the SENCo noted, would require an additional approach: challenging the typical 'discourse on using a teaching assistant, which is normally about presence rather than impact'. The SENCo's starting point had been to remind teachers that they were responsible for the engagement and learning of all pupils in their classes. He wanted the school to move away from a culture of using TAs to 'tick the box for inclusion'.

'[Teachers] feel like they can meet the needs of children with learning difficulties if there is another adult present. Not to do anything specifically, but simply to be there to have contact with that child. They feel like that ticks the box for meeting need; when we know that, not only is that not the case, but it can make things worse.'

Below we set out how schools can open up the TA role in the classroom by making simple changes to deployment routines. But school leaders need to lead the cultural change at the organisational level. Teachers must be encouraged to reconsider how they deploy TAs across attainment groups and how the school at large needs to abandon the discredited 'Velcro TA' model, where pupils with Statements are attached to a TA. Doing so reduces pupil separation from the teacher and creates authentic opportunities to increase both pupil independence and the amount of interaction they can have with teachers.

Teacher-level decisions

Teachers' deployment of TAs has implications for their own classroom practice. The challenge is to consider ways in which TAs can add value to what teachers do, in order to help them meet their responsibilities. In other words, to think first of all about what they should be doing to support lower-attaining pupils and those with SEN, and then to use the TA in ways to facilitate this. Teachers must organise their teaching in ways that mitigate the separation effect revealed through our research.

In the first instance, teachers need to question the notion of getting TAs to withdraw pupils from the class to work on tasks that are the same as, or differentiated from, what the rest of the class is doing. This was a common arrangement we have witnessed in many classrooms, and it must be avoided wherever possible.

In most cases, the changes teachers need to consider concern the use of TAs as an informal teaching resource for individual pupils and groups. Teachers need to reverse this situation: *they* must become the adult with whom pupils with SEN have regular, sustained and focused interactions. Rather than routinely assigning the TA to teach the pupils whose learning needs are the greatest and most demanding – and therefore require professional input – teachers will have to ensure the TA works with pupils across the class as a whole, thereby allowing them the opportunity to interact regularly with these pupils, and for sustained periods. Teachers in the EDTA project greatly improved and enriched their understanding of the learning needs and progress of pupils who previously worked more often with the TA than the teacher. We have observed similar improvements through our work with schools in the MITA programme.

This shift in TA deployment is fundamental, but as the teachers in the EDTA project found, it is not just beneficial, but relatively simple to implement. Their strategies reduced pupils' separation from them, from the curriculum, and from peers. Teachers can address the tendency for TAs to routinely support lower-attaining groups and pupils with SEN by widening the range of contexts in which they are deployed. Instead, use TAs to support groups of gifted and talented pupils, average-attaining pupils and mixed ability groups.

Teachers may even consider deploying themselves and their TA on a rotational basis, so both adults work with a different group each day throughout the week. One successful version of this model involves the teacher setting independent and group work tasks for the tables without an adult present, so over the course of the week, each table has the same amount of time being supported by the teacher, supported by the TA, working in a group and working independently.

During classwork, TAs tend to remain in one place working with a group or individual, while the teacher moves about the classroom, ensuring they are on-task and progressing; this is what we call 'roving'. Some schools have flipped the roles of the teacher and TA during classwork. One idea that gained broad support from teachers and TAs in the EDTA project was to use the roving TA to bring the teacher's attention particular individuals whom she saw were having difficulty with the task. Once alerted, the teacher moved in to provide targeted support while the TA continued to rove.

Depending on TAs' particular skills and their suitability to these roles, these ideas – all drawn from work undertaken in real classrooms – can be used in different combinations, depending on the lesson, the tasks and the needs of the pupils. Working with pupils in a pedagogical role across the attainment range, in a one-to-one, group or roving capacity, all present particular challenges. Therefore, such changes to the ways TAs are deployed will need to be accompanied by training. Indeed, moving to models of classroom organisation that provide more opportunities for teachers to work with pupils with SEN may require some specific training to raise teachers' knowledge and understanding of the needs of these pupils (e.g. particular types of SEN) and developing their pedagogical skills in this area.

At the core of the classroom deployment strategies that teachers use and develop must remain the notion that whatever pedagogical role is assigned to TAs, it should be monitored to ensure there is a fairer balance of teacher–pupil time across the attainment range, and that TAs are not being asked to work outside their current level of competency.

Case studies

Ensuring pupils with SEN get time with teachers I

SLT were concerned that some pupils with Statements of SEN, while included in the class, had proportionately less time with the teacher than other pupils. Too much of the curriculum was taught by a TA on a one-to-one basis. An appropriate balance of teacher and TA time was needed for pupils with SEN.

The school addressed this in three ways. Firstly, by ensuring that the expectation set out in the SEN Code of Practice – that class teachers are responsible for the progress of pupils with SEN – was reflected in the school's SEN policy. Secondly, by reviewing the amount of teacher time pupils with Statements received during the week. And finally, ensuring specific pupils had one-to-one or small group teaching from the SENCo each day.

As the school introduced these changes, there were concerns from parents of some Statemented pupils. They had different expectations of how support should be organised and were anxious that less time with the TA would be detrimental for their child. The school maintained a productive dialogue with parents to clarify the purpose and benefits of the new arrangements.

Ensuring pupils with SEN get time with teachers 2

The school tightened up on teachers' accountability for meeting the needs of pupils with SEN, embedding this principle of the Code of Practice into everyday classroom practice. The emphasis was on the needs of these pupils being met through high quality teaching, moving away from the model where TAs absorbed the primary responsibility for teaching. Pupil passports were introduced to ensure teachers had up-to-date information about the needs of the pupils in their class, so they could plan tasks appropriately.

Key recommendations on defining the pedagogical role of TAs

- Lead a whole-school drive to give up ineffective models of TA deployment in relation to pupils with SEN.
- Ensure this is a collaborative effort, and that teachers and TAs know SLT will support them through the process of change.
- Work towards a situation where the pupils with the greatest level of need have *at least* the same amount of time with teachers as their peers. Consider rotating the groups teachers and TAs work with across the week.
- Watch for the signs of ineffective deployment, such as evidence of pupil dependency on TAs (more on this in Chapter 5).
- Consider how teachers deploy themselves in lessons, in terms of the groups they tend to support.
- Ensure lower-attaining pupils and those with SEN are not routinely and unnecessarily separated from the teacher and the classroom.
- Consider additional classroom organisation strategies that do not require adult support; for example, peer-led group work.

TAs and intervention programmes

One of the commonplace ways in which TAs are deployed in a pedagogical role is to deliver intervention programmes in one-to-one or small group settings, away from the classroom. At worst, we have heard and seen for ourselves how the carousel of withdrawal for various interventions can amount to 'a lifestyle' for some pupils. The auditing process in one secondary school we worked with revealed, much to the headteacher's surprise, that pupils were being withdrawn from interventions to do interventions!

If TAs in your school are deployed to carry out intervention programmes and you intend to continue this form of the pedagogical role, then you will need to review all aspects of your current arrangements. As pupils are typically withdrawn from class for interventions, it should be a prerequisite of any TA-led programme that it *at least* compensates for time spent away from the teacher. Crucially, this does not mean we should pile the responsibility for pupils making accelerated progress on TAs. The SEN Code of Practice makes it clear that it is teachers who are responsible and accountable for pupil progress. Furthermore, interventions are not a substitute for consistently good teaching.

The Code also emphasises the use of evidence-based approaches to raising attainment. Therefore, it is essential you adopt well-structured interventions with reliable evidence of effectiveness. Which programme is used and how it is delivered is the key difference between effective and less effective use of TAs in aiding consistent and high-quality delivery. As a school, you need to review how intervention programmes are taught and how effective they are in fulfilling the overall learning needs of pupils.

Carrying out an 'interventions health check' will help you to identify any programmes that are ineffective, and would be ineffective regardless of who delivered them; sometimes it is the material that is the problem! We know schools that have evaluated the effectiveness of their interventions and dropped those that had little or no impact. As a consequence, these schools were in a position to reduce the number of out-of-class interventions taking place and shift towards a greater use of TAs in classrooms. Jean Gross's (2015) book, *Beating Bureaucracy in Special Educational Needs*, contains a useful toolkit for evaluating the quality of interventions. Below are some questions to ask when conducting your own health check.

Some important questions to ask about TAs and intervention programmes

- Do we select interventions that have a sound evidence base demonstrating success?
- Are we using good programmes badly?
- What are the aims and objectives of each of our intervention programmes?
- Do we know how well we achieve these aims and objectives with individual pupils?
- How do we track and evaluate pupil progress and the effectiveness of interventions?
- Do we ever adjust or even close down any ineffective programmes?
- Will TAs be asked to prepare the intervention sessions without input from the teachers of the pupils involved? If so, how do we justify this arrangement and ensure teachers are aware of the tasks and learning objectives of the intervention sessions?
- Will interventions be carried out during lesson time, meaning pupils are withdrawn from classroom learning? Which lessons will they be withdrawn from? And how often?
- How will teachers make best use of and extend learning from intervention sessions? How can they integrate this learning into whole-class contexts?

Primary school leaders should also consider whether the interventions are timely. Early intervention often has the most profound effect, so wherever possible, aim to identify learning needs and address them through the appropriate strategies before pupils leave Key Stage 1.

In Chapter 1 we described how TAs can have a positive impact on pupil progress when they are used to deliver interventions, and the clear conditions needed for success. On the basis of the evidence currently available (Higgins et al. 2013), there are only a handful of programmes in the UK for which there is secure evidence of effectiveness. If your school is using or considering using programmes that are 'unproven' and possibly unstructured, ensure they include the common elements of effective interventions:

- Sessions are brief (20–50 minutes), occur regularly (3–5 times per week) and are maintained over a sustained period (8–20 weeks). Careful timetabling is in place to enable consistent delivery.
- TAs receive extensive training from experienced trainers and/or teachers (5–30 hours per intervention).
- The intervention has structured supporting resources and lesson plans, with clear objectives and possibly a delivery script.
- Ensure there is fidelity to the programme and do not depart from suggested delivery protocols. If it says deliver every other day for 30 minutes to groups of no more than four pupils, do this!
- Likewise, ensure TAs closely follow the plan and structure of the intervention, and use delivery scripts.
- Assessments are used to identify appropriate pupils, guide areas for focus and track pupils' progress. Effective interventions ensure the right support is being provided to the right pupil.
- Ensure connections are made between the out-of-class learning in the intervention and classroom teaching.

(taken from Sharples et al. 2015)

There are a number of commercially available interventions programmes that offer a layered approach to delivery, with a component designed to be delivered by teachers and a less technical sister programme designed to be delivered by TAs. Such programmes involve the teacher working with the lowest-attaining pupils and the TA working with the pupils in the tier above; with those who are struggling, but not as in need of the teacher's more advanced pedagogical input as the lowest attainers. You may be able to remodel existing interventions in a similar way, but do not overlook the need for both teachers and TAs to have specialist training.

Once choices have been made about which intervention programmes the school will use, teachers can be given the responsibility of managing the intervention programmes. In secondary schools, giving English and mathematics departments the responsibility for coordinating the day-to-day roles of TAs will help ensure teachers have full control of the factors they need to plan effective provision. In primary schools, teachers should be supported to capitalise on TA-led learning by aligning the content of strategically selected intervention programmes with wider coverage of literacy and numeracy.

Finally, bear in mind that withdrawal from class to do interventions can be a cause of resentment, meaning that pupils are not in the best frame of mind to learn. Avoid removing pupils from lessons they enjoy (such as art) or activities (e.g. assemblies) that make them feel excluded.

Teacher-level decisions

The DISS project called attention to the widespread lack of teacher involvement with, and general ignorance of, the content, teaching and outcomes of TA-led intervention programmes. The purpose of any intervention must be to produce a pay off in terms of improving overall end-of-year attainment in an area of weakness (e.g. reading). A surer route to achieving this is the greater involvement of teachers in the preparation and delivery of interventions. It is important that where TAs deliver interventions, teachers do not become detached from the broad aims and effectiveness of the programmes used and the specific content and objectives of individual sessions. Given that teachers are responsible for learning outcomes, they need to have a stake in:

- The selection, preparation and assessment of interventions.
- Decisions about where and when TAs deliver the programmes. If pupils need to be withdrawn from lessons, which lessons will they be withdrawn from?
- Ensuring the quality and effectiveness of teaching approaches used by TAs.
- Possible involvement in the delivery of interventions; for example, via the layered approach described above.
- Establishing a process of specific and (at least) weekly feedback from TAs on pupil performance.
- Integrating and extending the learning gained from intervention sessions in whole-class input and work with individuals and groups.

Interventions tend to be quite separate (physically and pedagogically) from classroom activities and the lack of time for teachers and TAs to liaise means there is relatively little connection between what pupils experience in and away from the classroom. To capitalise on the coverage of TA-led interventions, teachers need to ensure explicit connections are made between learning experiences in different contexts. Findings from the DISS and MAST studies found teachers were not consistent in their attempts to provide this 'bridging across'. It can often be left to pupils to make links between the coverage of the intervention and the wider curriculum coverage back in the classroom. Given they are the pupils who find accessing learning difficult in the first place, this presents a huge additional challenge.

In terms of delivery, teachers could explore the prospect of delivering an intervention session in the classroom, while the TA roves or supervises the class. We have found in cases where teachers and TAs have been trained together, there is a greater integration of the learning achieved by pupils in the intervention sessions with their wider classroom experience.

Either way, the key is for teachers to view the intervention from the pupils' point of view and ensure they enrich their learning experiences, building on and making relevant the time spent out of class. When teachers have greater awareness of pupils' learning from interventions, they can draw on concepts, facts, skills and understanding developed in the withdrawal sessions into their lesson planning, and, when pupils return to lessons, ask questions that help them apply, demonstrate and consolidate new learning.

Case study

Integrating interventions with classwork

One TA had a heavy responsibility for leading intervention programmes for pupils in Year 3 and Year 6 classes. She explained that the Year 6 mathematics content matched what the pupils were doing in class with their teacher, and that the teacher knew the learning objectives and sequence of lessons in the intervention programme. This allowed her to synchronise and integrate learning from the two contexts. In contrast, the Year 3 teacher knew nothing of the intervention programme that the TA led with pupils from her class and so there is no integration of learning.

The integration of specific programmes with the mainstream curriculum, together with the alignment with pupils' curriculum targets, is vital to building on the positive gains that research has shown can be obtained by deploying TAs to deliver quality interventions.

Key recommendations on interventions

- Carry out a systematic evaluation of all the interventions you use. Based on this evaluation, be willing to change the location, frequency, content and duration of interventions. Ditch any interventions not producing benefits for pupils.
- Ensure teachers are informed about the interventions used and that the selection of a specific programme aligns with pupils' individual needs and their curriculum targets.
- Encourage teachers to have a greater stake and involvement in the selection, preparation, delivery and assessment of intervention programmes.
- Make sure teachers plan sessions with TAs, and be mindful of when and where they take place.
- Ensure teachers obtain regular feedback from TAs on pupil performance in interventions and use this to inform their lesson planning and classroom interactions.

TAs leading classes

Some of the schools we visited as part of the DISS project (and many more who provided responses to our questionnaires) deployed TAs to lead classes as part of arrangements to release teachers for preparation, planning and assessment (PPA) time or to cover short-term teacher absences. In secondary schools, cover supervisors often undertake lesson cover for unplanned teacher absences. Much of what we have to say in this section (and indeed throughout much of the book) can be applied to support staff working in this role.

One of the most contentious issues arising out of the National Agreement was TAs leading classes. In a very visible way, TAs were seen to replace teachers, even though the nature of the work – labelled 'supervision' – was described in such a way as to make it distinct from 'teaching'. However, from our research on the DISS project, it was clear that when TAs led classes, they took on a teaching role, much as they did when they were working with individuals or groups. In many cases, this was inevitable, as pupils keen to get on with the work left for them by the teacher asked TAs questions relating to tasks and for explanations or clarifications of concepts.

Leading classes gives the TA a role that very obviously overlaps with that of the teacher, in terms of having class-level responsibilities and interactions. The aim of the restructuring process described in this book is to create roles for TAs that are distinct from the teachers' role and responsibilities, and so you must be absolutely clear about your expectations of what TAs can and cannot do, and what you want them to achieve, if they are deployed to lead classes.

If you decide to deploy TAs in roles that put them in charge of classes in the absence of a teacher, you must be very deliberate in your choice of the individual(s) to whom you assign this role. You may even wish to assign a pair of TAs to lead a class, so they can support one another. Although a process of training for TAs may be necessary for some TAs who do not, at present, have the full skills set to thrive in the role in which you wish to place them, the supervision role is something of a special case. It is likely that leading classes will not be something every TA in your school will wish to do; it takes a particular level of confidence to command a class of 30 pupils, especially if the culture of behaviour and/or respect for adults in the school is not all it could be. TAs we have spoken to as part of the DISS and EDTA projects describe the damage to their confidence sustained by comments from pupils that undermine their authority and position; for instance: 'You're not a proper teacher'.

Primary school leaders could consider developing a specific TA role along the lines of a cover supervisor to take on lesson cover and/or PPA cover more or less full time. You should identify the TA(s) in your school who are willing to take on this role – and make them able. Accreditation against the HLTA standards can be used as a benchmark for determining an individual's competence in leading whole classes.

The evidence from the DISS project is quite clear: the effectiveness of TAs and cover supervisors hinges on the quality of preparation provided; not just in terms of training in classroom management, but also in terms of wider systems for sharing lesson information. We return to this in Chapter 6.

Key recommendations on TAs leading classes

- Ask yourself: will pupils accept TAs leading classes? Is the climate conducive to this kind of role in our school?
- Be absolutely clear about the limitations of TAs deployed to lead classes. They are *not* teachers, so calibrate your expectations accordingly. Ensure teachers are clear on this too.
- Consider creating a designated 'cover TA' role for your strongest TA(s).

Class-based, year-based or subject-based TAs

The allocation of TAs to particular classes, year groups or subjects is necessarily a school-level decision made by you and your SLT. Having established the effectiveness of the present model of TA deployment across the school and its alignment with your values and aims via your audit, some changes are likely.

As we have said previously, there is no 'one size fits all' approach, and your school may require a mix of the broad models of TA deployment we describe here. For example, if you are in a primary school, it may be more appropriate to have class-based TAs in Key Stage 1 and TAs that work across Key Stage 2 classes in a particular year or years. If you run a large secondary school, you may even consider having your most knowledgeable TAs attached to subjects to support Key Stage 4 pupils in the build-up to exams. Whatever you decide, we strongly recommend all efforts are made to move away from the so-called 'Velcro model'. Here, we look in turn at deployment for TAs who are predominantly based in classes, year groups and subject departments.

Class-based TAs

A school system where TAs are allocated to classes presents some advantages. Continuity, for example, means there is greater opportunity for the teacher–TA partnership to develop. It also allows adults to become more familiar with the pupils' attitudes to learning and behaviour, and their particular learning needs.

However, findings from the DISS project and the MAST study revealed some potential disadvantages for teachers and pupils from this model of deployment. First, we found teachers could avoid taking direct responsibility for some aspects of their teaching, in terms of leaving tasks to be prepared and taught by TAs, especially interventions. Second, we discovered there is a risk teachers assume TAs are so familiar with the way they work, that explanations or explicit expectations are not required. This failure to make the tacit knowledge teachers possess explicit to TAs impedes TAs' capacity to work in ways that advance pupil learning.

You will need to alert teachers who work with class-based TAs about the potential dangers of separation from teachers, and support them to develop alternative ways of deploying TAs. Leaving individual teachers to make choices in isolation is not adequate, and such practice has unquestionably led to the situation described in the DISS project, where there is a distinct lack of coordination and consistency in TA use across the school; in secondary schools this issue is particularly acute. Your school policy should be clear on how class-based TAs are to be deployed.

TEACHER-LEVEL DECISIONS

We have already touched on some of the models of class-level deployment in the section on TAs and pupils with SEN, in terms of TAs roving the room and working with different attainment groups. So here we look at the other ways in which teachers can make the most of class-based TAs on the basis of findings from the EDTA project and our MITA programme, which show significant benefits can be derived from making simple changes to how they are deployed.

Firstly, simply having an awareness of the impact of ineffective forms of TA deployment means teachers are much more mindful of reducing their use of these models. Teachers who often send or allow TAs to work with individuals and groups outside the class do this far less.

Secondly, teachers use the three-part lesson structure (teacher input, main learning task and plenary) to deploy TAs in different ways. Before changes were made as part of the EDTA project, our pre-intervention data revealed that when TAs were in the classroom, teachers spent more than half of their time talking to the whole class. During these times, TAs were 'passive': listening to the teacher teach, and having brief intermittent interactions with pupils. In the MAST study, for each hour observed, TAs were found to be passive for 20 minutes. As one participant in the EDTA project told us:

> If you're just kind of not doing anything, and the teacher's stood there reading from a book and things like that, and then they'll start asking the class questions … you can't really do an awful lot, can you? If that goes on for near enough the whole lesson, what can you do?
>
> (Secondary TA)

Once this was brought to teachers' attention, they did things differently in a bid to make better use of TAs' time during their input. Some teachers deployed the TA in a more prominent role during their input, ensuring they had been prepared in advance. In one primary classroom, the TA took notes on the whiteboard, allowing the teacher to remain facing the class and more able to identify pupils who showed signs of not understanding the concept or task, and to respond to any off-task, inattentive behaviour she would have missed with her back turned.

Case studies

An enhanced role for TAs 1

The TA in one secondary classroom had been given a more prominent role at the front of the class, and did tasks for the teacher, such as writing notes on the whiteboard and asking pre-prepared questions in turn with the teacher. This form of deployment had two notable effects. First, the notes on the board were made primarily for the benefit of a pupil in the class with dyslexia, which avoided the often stigmatising effect of the TA sitting beside him taking notes for him; plus it began to reverse the tendency for him to depend on the TA, and gave him the opportunity and independence to practise his handwriting. Second, the small, well-defined role the TA had in lesson delivery allowed her to display her significant subject knowledge, thus challenging the view held by some pupils in the class that the TA was 'less knowledgeable' than the teacher.

An enhanced role for TAs 2

TAs in one primary school had received training in team teaching approaches. They were encouraged to be part of the shared writing process and to deliver lesson starters, while the teacher worked with targeted children. When modelling writing at the front of the class, TAs wrote on the board as the teacher dictated.

TAs also made intentional errors that pupils had to identify unprompted. The mistakes had been identified in the pupils' own work and discussed with the TA prior to the lesson. As a result of training and support, TAs reported feeling more confident to stand in front of the class and felt their profile has been raised within the classrooms. 'What we have successfully managed to create are "teaching teams", where all the adults are equal in the eyes of the children', reported the deputy headteacher.

Some teachers made a more conscious effort to model good teaching or questioning for TAs during their input. TAs made notes on keywords, relevant questions and instructional techniques to use when working with a group during the main learning task. This is in stark contrast to the common picture we found in the DISS project, where TAs are expected to 'tune in' to the teacher's classroom talk and make their own decisions about what is needed to support pupils with tasks. Several teachers instructed TAs to watch and take notes on a particular pupil, or to observe peer-to-peer interactions. This information was later fed back to the teacher.

The lesson plenaries we observed tended to be quite short. Often, TAs continued to work with an individual or group, or collected in resources. As plenaries are whole-class, teacher-led sessions, some of the suggestions relating to TA deployment during the main input may apply here (e.g. TAs scribing on the whiteboard).

Year-based TAs

It may be that you choose to allocate TAs to year groups or Key Stages, rather than classes. Some year groups may merit a greater number of TAs, or more TA time. These considerations will be part of your deployment decision-making process and you should clearly explain and justify your rationale for these choices to the teachers working in each year group.

Year-based TAs have the advantage of becoming familiar with the curriculum content, schemes of work, expected range of pupil outcomes and forms of assessment designed for the year group to which they are attached. There may be other aspects, such as models of classroom organisation and expected levels of pupil independence, with which TAs can become conversant, and which will be consistent across all the classes in the year. In secondary schools, the spread of pupil attainment is likely to widen over Key Stages 3 and 4 (and with it, the demands of their tasks), so allocation to a single year group might be more appropriate.

If you deploy TAs across several classes, you will need to reflect this in the amount of pre-lesson preparation time you allocate. Discussions with year-group teachers can benefit all concerned because it opens up the chances of sharing planning, preparation of resources, coverage of the schemes of work, as well as developing the new models of TA deployment. TAs are well positioned to act as conduits to inform teachers about how different pupils behave and their progress in different lessons, with different teachers.

Subject-based TAs

Secondary schools operate a departmental structure, organising teaching and assessment into curriculum subjects, both discretely (e.g. mathematics) and in groups (e.g. expressive arts). It may be your choice to allocate TAs to departments and leave the detailed decisions regarding how individual TAs are deployed within each subject to your heads of department, through consultation with their staff. However, the school policy on TA deployment must explicitly set the parameters for middle leader-level decision-making, setting out the criteria for such decisions, along with clear expectations for how the TAs can be used by teachers to aid pupil progress. It must also be clear on how TAs are *not* to be used.

The advantages for secondary schools of deploying TAs in this way are fairly self-evident: there is a narrower range of subject content with which to be conversant; the same is true of the syllabus, set texts, assessment criteria and examination formats; and there are fewer pupils to teach each week, so familiarity with them and their needs is that much easier.

TAs in schools we know that have moved to this model are also much more likely to be included in the life of the department, and are welcomed to department meetings. Closer working partnerships are nurtured through various forms of professional development and team meetings. Subject-based TAs reported being fully included in the life of the department and are valued members of the team. Teachers can also become more used to planning for, and working in collaboration with, individual TAs who will regularly be deployed in their classrooms. Growing knowledge of, and trust in, the qualities and abilities of departmental TAs can be a benefit to teachers and pupils alike.

In developing this school-level model of TA deployment, you will need to consider issues of the suitability of individuals (in terms of their level of subject knowledge) and preparedness for a teaching role (in terms of their pedagogical knowledge). It should not be assumed that having a degree in a particular subject means TAs will be effective teachers of it. For TAs located in English and mathematics departments, training to deliver specific literacy and numeracy interventions may be necessary.

Case studies

Subject-based TAs 1

One secondary school in the EDTA project restructured its use of TAs, moving from a model of deployment where TAs operated from a physically separated Learning Support provision and supporting pupils with SEN across the curriculum, to a model where TAs were based in subject departments in the main school building. The TAs who participated in the project were two of only a small number of TAs who had been subject-based for at least one year already, and acted as advocates for the benefits of being located within a faculty (e.g. in terms of greater opportunities for communicating with teachers and building deeper subject knowledge).

Subject-based TAs 2

Another secondary school trialled allocating TAs to smaller departments. Heads of department decided how TAs would be deployed in classes, not always supporting pupils with SEN. Support was more targeted where TAs were familiar and confident in a particular subject. Drawing on TAs' expertise brought them considerable job satisfaction. Additionally, TAs got to know more pupils across the school and vice versa. There were more naturally occurring opportunities to plan with teachers and TAs were encouraged to attend departmental meetings. Support with behaviour management improved and in some cases TAs ran clubs related to the subject area.

Subject-based TAs 3

One large secondary school that moved to a faculty-based deployment system found that this created more opportunities to liaise with teachers: 'After one term we can already see gains across many areas. TAs have more time to liaise with their faculties; after school, during weekly morning briefings and fortnightly after school meetings'.

Key recommendations class-based, year-based or subject-based TAs

- The model of the Velcro TA is no longer an option. Explore alternative ways of deploying TAs in predominantly class-based, year group-based or subject department-based roles.
- Be mindful of the risks associated with class-based models in particular (e.g. pupils' dependency on TAs and separation from the teacher).
- Ensure the deployment decisions that will be devolved to teachers and/or heads of department are clearly framed within your school policy on TA deployment, and set the expectations and limits of what is acceptable. This will greatly enhance the coordination and consistency of TA use across the school.
- Ensure a consistent approach to TA deployment where they work across one or more classes, and capitalise on the useful information TAs pick up about pupils when working across classes or subjects.
- Teachers: be aware of the occasions when the TA(s) in your class are passive. Does this add value to your teaching? Consider how to use TAs in different parts of the lesson, perhaps to aid classroom control or to pick up on specific information relevant to teaching and support. Their role can vary from lesson to lesson.
- Be aware that deploying TAs across a greater number of classes/teachers will have implications for the amount of time needed for pre- and post-lesson communication.

TAs' conditions of employment and TA recruitment

The DISS project found that decisions about TAs' contracts and hours of work had a strong bearing on how TAs were deployed and prepared, and this is captured in the WPR model. So, once your school has reviewed its deployment decisions, based on the most relevant and important criteria, it may be that the issues of recruitment and conditions of employment are also found to be in need of attention.

The job description associated with each type of TA role will demand different sets of recruitment and selection criteria. Auditing your present TA workforce will reveal strengths and also gaps, which should feed directly into your recruitment process. In particular, decisions about what TAs in pedagogical roles are employed to achieve will need to be made prior to setting out job descriptions and adding new recruits to the TA workforce.

The specific nature of any vacant TA roles you are seeking to fill must be made explicit in adverts and recruitment materials. The selection criteria must be clear in terms of the qualifications and skills, as well as experience (if applicable), the appointment will be based. For pedagogical roles, the interview process must also reflect the emphasis on teaching. Many candidates who in the past may have been appointed, or thought suitable to be TAs, will be seen in a new light with these tighter, more demanding criteria being applied.

We have termed this new approach to TA recruitment as 'year zero', meaning schools are resetting the clock and will henceforth select TAs according to more rigorous standards. A new breed of TAs may be what your school needs, and new recruits are an ideal way to face this reality and raise the bar by setting minimum entry levels to the role. As a result of participation in the EDTA project, a number of the schools set minimum expectations for qualifications for new appointees. We know of many schools that will only consider graduates for vacant TA posts, which may have been prompted by the recent and rapid growth of academies.[4]

But by choosing to give TAs a pedagogical role, you are obligated to be mindful about their competence as unqualified teachers. Setting the bar for entry in this way puts greater emphasis on the teaching the school expects TAs to carry out. It makes explicit what has previously been implicit; teaching pupils requires drawing on one's knowledge, understanding and skills. Previously, this reality was neglected. As many headteachers told us in the DISS project, they tended to make appointments based on impressions and assumptions that successful candidates 'had what it takes'; rarely did they describe anything more rigorous. If we are serious about raising the esteem of the TA workforce, this second-rate approach to recruitment must end.

The TAs who are currently in post may present you with some particular challenges. A review and possible changes to job descriptions must be carried out in order for the school to address TAs' levels of preparedness, particularly for those with a pedagogical role. If you are unable to align some individuals with certain roles, changes in deployment will be necessary.

As we have already noted, the process of reform is likely to include dispensing with certain roles that exist at present. You may find yourself in a position where some of the TAs in your school do not, at present, have the competencies to fill the roles you want to establish. Or some TAs may not wish to fulfill the role you have in mind. This will be a matter for the individual. We do not underestimate the fact that there may

Case study

Raising the bar

One primary school that participated in the EDTA project has seen the quality of applicants for TA vacancies greatly improve, due to the way in which posts are advertised. There is a stronger set of expectations set out from the start: job descriptions are much clearer and the interview process is more rigorous. The induction process has been improved, with training provided by the HLTAs. There is a formal system of performance management in place for TAs, which includes an audit. TAs who do well are being used to provide peer support through observation. The school has become a beacon of good practice, visited by staff from nearby schools. The experience has been good for TAs' morale.

In another primary school, where only graduates were considered for TA posts, a rigorous interview and selection process has been put in place. In addition to a formal interview with the headteacher and SENCo, candidates have to sit the Year 6 spelling, punctuation and grammar test, a mental mathematics test, and undertake a practical teaching task with a group of pupils.

be difficult choices involved in undertaking the systemic programme of restructuring we are advocating in this book. But as educationalists, we have to put the needs of pupils first. If redundancies are likely, we recommend you seek advice.

However, we stress it is the *roles* that are to be done away with, not the individuals who occupy them. In fairness to TAs, the role has historically grown around them and this has not been accompanied with the necessary support to help them adjust. This is why we would advocate a process of training to support TAs to grow into the new roles you create.

In support of this more professionalised approach to managing and organising TAs, there is one further consideration worth mentioning here. We deal with changes to improve TA preparation in Chapter 6, but taking preparedness seriously will often necessitate changes to working hours. You may need to extend TAs' working day at the start, the end or both, and this may be problematic for some individuals. Again, these are matters it will be up to individuals to deal with. TAs who accept this new arrangement are likely to require new or updated contracts of employment, starting from the next school year. For new recruits, the hours of work you wish to introduce can be made clear during the application process, so they are able to make an informed choice about whether they would be willing to accept the conditions of employment associated with the role.

The school policy on TAs should express clearly what the TA roles are, what the selection criteria must be and include examples of the job descriptions for the roles you create. Teachers and TAs should all be fully aware of the policy, so deployment decisions, preparation and performance review processes are all integrated in order to maximise the effectiveness of TAs' contributions to pupils' learning.

Key recommendations on TAs' conditions of employment and TA recruitment

- Adopt a 'year zero' approach to TA recruitment. Approach future recruitment of TAs differently, raising the entry-level qualifications and making the hours of work clear.
- These arrangements should be formally expressed in a job description and person specification. The new standards and expectations should be defined by, and set out in, the school's TA policy.
- Conditions of employment will need to be reviewed for existing TAs and for all future contracts, particularly those relating to changes to working hours.
- Make every effort to train TAs who are currently in post if they do not possess the full skills set required for the role in which you wish to deploy them.

The choices and decisions you and your SLT make to affect school-level change should be seen as an outcome of the desire to make TAs more effective in enhancing pupils' progress.

Summary

In the last chapter of this book, we report the findings from evaluations of the EDTA project and the MITA programme on the main effects of introducing the alternative models of TA deployment we have described here. We end this chapter by noting that a growing number of schools have addressed TA deployment to such an extent they have turned around, or are beginning to reverse, the main effects of TA deployment identified in the DISS project:

- Pupils who are typically supported by TAs (e.g. lower-attaining pupils and those with SEN) experience less separation from the classroom, the curriculum and their teachers.
- Lower-attaining pupils and those with SEN receive more input and support from teachers, either individually or as part of a group.
- At the same time, teachers are able to learn more about individual pupils' learning weaknesses and their potential.
- Teachers make better use of TAs in lessons.
- Pupils' dependency on TA support is reduced.

Notes

1 For information, visit http://www.elsanetwork.org
2 Structured conversations form part of the *Achievement for All* intervention package. For more information, visit www.afa3as.org.uk
3 For more information, visit www.triplep.net/glo-en/home/
4 The freedom schools have in order to apply such stipulations varies between local authorities. If in doubt, seek advice from your authority's human resources department.

Chapter 5

The practice of TAs

Introduction

Few would disagree that the quality of verbal interactions between adults and pupils is at the heart of effective teaching and learning. This chapter focuses on the nature and quality of TA-to-pupil interactions.

The DISS project found schools were largely unaware that TAs' interactions with pupils tended to focus on task completion rather than understanding, and that compared with teachers, TAs asked more closed questions and fewer open questions, thereby closing down learning opportunities. Schools were equally unaware of the problems TAs faced when it came to carrying out the tasks delegated to them by teachers. Consequently, teachers and school leaders were generally unable to detect possible limitations, or even damage, to pupils' learning and progress.

There is an impoverished understanding in some schools about the quality and effectiveness of TA practice that cannot remain unchallenged. Having made decisions about the roles of TAs, you must address how this manifests itself in TAs' interactions with pupils, especially where TAs are positioned in instructional roles.

However, there remains a clear and major distinction between TAs with teaching roles, for whom it is necessary to have interactions concerning subject content and learning, and TAs employed predominantly in non-pedagogical roles, who have a different, but complementary, impact on learning.

If you have decided TAs will have a pedagogical role in your school – working directly with pupils, delivering and supporting curriculum content – then the issue of TAs' practice must be addressed in a rigorous and systematic way. The key question to begin with is: how much do you already know about the nature and quality of TAs' interactions with pupils? As we advise in Chapter 2, some form of auditing should precede and inform changes to TAs' practice. The insight obtained from close attention to TAs' talk is both essential and extremely valuable. Effective changes aimed at improving the quality of talk, in terms of promoting pupil learning, will only be possible if you are well informed about present practice.

In this chapter, we look at the implications for TAs in pedagogical roles concerning the second main component of the Wider Pedagogical Role model: practice. Specifically, we focus on two dimensions of talk that emerged from the EDTA project and are of interest to many of the schools that participate in the MITA programme: (i) effective questioning skills; and (ii) supporting and developing pupils' independent learning skills.

We make reference at the end to our sister publication, *The Teaching Assistant's Guide To Effective Interaction: How to Maximise Your Impact* (Bosanquet, Radford and Webster 2016), which contains detailed guidance on how TAs can develop a role as effective scaffolders of learning, consistent with our coverage here on encouraging the type of practice that can grow pupils' independence.

Some important questions to ask about TA-to-pupil interactions

- How much do you already know about the nature and quality of TAs' interactions with pupils?
- Do you attempt to monitor TAs' talk with pupils; for example, their use of questions?
- How would you respond if you discovered TAs frequently provided pupils with answers, or misled them (unintentionally) with inaccurate information?

TAs' questioning skills

Learning interactions largely involve questioning. Asking questions to engage and promote learning is a skilled task. Such pedagogical questions are generally categorised as closed or open, or as lower-order or higher-order, with open and higher-order questions regarded as the more effective types of talk (see Table 2.5 in Chapter 2).

The DISS project findings revealed pupils are engaged in sustained and active interactions with TAs far more often than they are with teachers. But our analyses of adult-to-pupil talk (including questioning) also showed marked differences in the quality of TA-to-pupil interactions when compared with teacher-to-pupil interactions. TA talk is often of a poorer quality: it is less cognitively demanding and task completion is prioritised over learning and understanding (see Blatchford et al. 2012b).

As questioning is essential to developing pupils' thinking, aiding the growth of their conceptual knowledge and understanding, extending their skills for critical thinking and checking their learning while engaged in tasks, we think there should be a concerted drive to improve TAs' questioning skills. If your audit reveals TAs' talk is characterised by closed and lower-order questions, you need to take action to raise the quality of their questioning skills. Of course, closed questions have their place in teaching, but you should be alert to their overuse or use where an open question is more appropriate to the task. Many of the participants in the EDTA project admitted at the outset to giving little consideration to TAs' questioning techniques:

> Without realising it I was quite often using closed questions ... A lot of the time, because the kids I'm working with often struggle, you just want them to feel like they're progressing or achieving. But actually, when you think about it, for that minute or second when you've virtually given them the answer, they might be feeling a bit better, but if you look at the big picture, it's not helping their progress.
>
> (Secondary TA)

If you recognise this situation, you should raise the awareness of the importance of questioning, provide TAs with models of good practice, and support them in developing their questioning skills.

Raising awareness

Skilful questioning to aid learning is, by its nature, a two-way transaction. Interactions are designed to lift the lid on the workings of the pupil's mind; to reveal to both the teacher and the pupil just what is known, how much is properly understood, and where any barriers to learning may be. This is the vital role of questioning, and until it is brought to their attention, most TAs may be unaware of its importance and how demanding it is to handle effectively.

School leaders should consider training all TAs in effective questioning techniques. Many schools we work with deliver this training in-house. When the training is led by a senior leader with extensive classroom experience, it sends a message to TAs (and teachers) about the seriousness and value of this skill. The key is for TAs to develop an understanding of questioning techniques that help them to push pupils' learning on. What is required is very clear, practical advice and guidance on what effective questioning looks like and when it should be applied.

Case study

Focusing on the importance of quality questioning

One primary school put a deliberate focus on questioning, which sent out a powerful message about the esteem in which the school held it. The deputy headteacher led training for TAs on suitable questioning techniques. These techniques complemented the questioning techniques used by class teachers. Pairs of TAs observed one another working with pupils and made notes for a feedback discussion. TAs appreciated the opportunity to learn from one another and to develop new skills and practical strategies.

Developing models of good practice

Teachers are well placed to provide TAs with models of good questioning via their whole-class input. TAs are familiar with listening to teachers teach and some have no doubt picked up useful skills from their observations. However, because they lack the proper guidance, many TAs may engage superficially with what they see and hear in the classroom. The deeper intentions, selection of forms and various uses of the questions – tacit as they are to teachers – are less likely to be understood and used systematically by TAs.

Opportunities to model good questioning practice and formative assessment techniques are available every time a TA works in a class alongside a teacher. As we suggested in Chapter 4, if teachers are clear about what they want TAs to do at different stages of the lesson, they can create the opportunity for TAs to observe their whole-class input and take note of particular techniques they use, which TAs can use later as they support individuals or groups. Teachers will need to be clear about which techniques they want TAs to adopt in, say, their group-work, because not all forms of questioning which teachers use in their whole-class talk will be relevant to contexts in which TAs mainly work. Teachers could arrange for TAs to observe them working with individuals and groups, and model the questioning techniques that are effective in these contexts.

TAs should note the variety of questions and the use of thinking time, and use this to reflect on their own practice. Attention can also be given as to how teachers manage instances where a pupil does not know the answer, or gives an incorrect or incomplete answer, and how the teacher stimulates and prompts pupils to generate ideas.

Case study

Modelling questioning

In one primary school, a TA observed the teacher working one-to-one with a pupil with SEN. The teacher's interactions involved a lot of questioning, probing and scaffolding. The teacher and TA discussed the observation afterwards. The TA gained useful insights into working effectively with pupils one-to-one. She identified instances where the teacher's actions had been particularly effective and different to what she would have done. For example, the TA noted how the teacher gave the pupil ample time to respond to her questions. The TA realised that she did not tend to allow as much time.

Resources

Questions for TAs to ask pupils can be included in teachers' lessons plans and given to TAs in advance. Teachers could also prepare questions or prompts linked to subjects. Of course, as TAs develop their questioning skills over time, and this becomes a regular feature of their practice, there will be less need to provide detailed direction.

Some teachers in the EDTA project provided TAs with frameworks and examples of different types of questions and prompts designed to facilitate learning and critical thinking, some of which were based on Bloom's taxonomy. With the kind permission of the teachers who developed them, we have reproduced these resources in Appendices 4 and 5. There are downloadable versions available on our website.

A popular resource is the simple-to-use question matrix shown in Table 5.1. Question openers of increasing complexity can be constructed using a word from further down the left-hand column and a word from further along the top row. For example, comprehension or recall questions beginning with 'who is' or 'what did' are of a lower order than questions beginning with 'why would' or 'how might', which invite speculation.

Table 5.1 Effective question matrix

		Complexity				
	Is ...	Did ...	Can ...	Would ...	Will ...	Might ...
Who						
What						
Where						
Why						
When						
How						

(left axis label: Complexity, with downward arrow)

Case studies

Avoiding unproductive questions

One teacher gave her TA written guidance on unproductive questions, which err towards spoon-feeding, 'over-prompting' and task completion. In this way, the TA was as aware of less effective techniques as she was of effective techniques. Examples of the former include:

- *Recall questions* to which the answer is obvious
- *Rhetorical questions* solely for dramatic effect
- *Yes or No questions* that inhibit discussion
- *Leading questions* that are not open-ended
- *'Guess what I'm thinking' questions* where you have already formulated the answer you want or expect
- *'Why don't you try ...' questions* that supply alternative answers or ideas

Using a question bank

TAs and teachers in one school developed a question bank: a laminated resource listing categories of useful questions. Use of the question bank encouraged greater variety in questioning techniques with pupils. Members of the SLT had referred to the bank during observations, helping to gauge TAs' range and use of questions.

TAs in another school used a similar resource, developed by a secondary school English teacher. The teacher encouraged teachers and TAs across the department to use a prototype version, and used their comments and feedback to produce an improved version.

Embedding and sustaining practice

Our research has revealed TAs have little or no choice about the ways in which they are deployed. Our wider understanding of the TA role shows this is a historical development, which has remained unchallenged for years. Given this context, it should be noted that undoing old habits and replacing them with effective questioning skills will take time. Schools in the EDTA project recognised that developing more effective questioning skills required changing deeply embedded practices, and this situation is echoed in many of the schools we work with as part of the MITA programme. Asking closed questions is an ingrained practice, as is the tendency to jump in automatically with additional questions, rather than allowing time for a pupil to respond to the first question. Therefore, school leaders and teachers must recognise this and monitor TAs' progress. They should follow up initial training with further opportunities to practise and on-going mentoring and support. Such training and support should also be part of the school induction process for new TAs.

TAs should be encouraged to appraise their own practice critically and have open discussions with teachers aimed at developing a shared understanding of the purpose of talk and the desired outcomes. In particular, TAs must be convinced that task completion is not the primary objective, and that the priority must be on talk that advances learning. This was certainly something of a revelation for the participants in the EDTA project, who, once exposed to the findings from the DISS study, were convinced of the need to eradicate ineffective and unhelpful forms of interaction and replace them with more constructive models. One TA explained it is difficult to break habits, but awareness of one's own practice and the implications of using restricted forms of talk is a critical first step in self-improvement: 'I caught myself saying [to a pupil] the other day, "Why don't you use x word, instead of y word?" And I think, "Oh God, I shouldn't be saying that!"'

Finally, once the practice has become embedded, school leaders should ensure use of questioning is reviewed as part of TAs' annual performance appraisal. This will send a strong signal that the school expects TAs to demonstrate effective use of questions in support of pupils' learning and to work on continuously improving this aspect of their practice.

Case study

Monitoring implementation

TAs received training on the use of talk to extend pupils' speaking and listening skills, and to develop their writing skills. The aim was to enable pupils to work with a greater level of independence and to prevent TAs giving them the answers. Observations carried out by teaching staff showed that TAs were more aware of how they questioned pupils. Some TAs were confident about asking questions and withdrew to allow pupils to work without further support. Some pupils, mainly in Key Stage 4, were less reliant on the TAs to give them answers. Other TAs found it difficult to strike the appropriate balance.

Key recommendations on TAs' questioning skills

- Make a concerted drive to ensure TA-to-pupil interactions promote thinking and learning, rather than task completion.
- Raise awareness among both teachers and TAs of the importance of quality questioning.
- Teachers need to share their tacit knowledge and skills relating to effective pupil interactions with TAs via training, observations and discussions.
- Ensure teachers explicitly model key techniques in their whole-class input, so TAs' practice is consistent with that of teachers when supporting pupils.
- Produce resources with exemplars of quality questioning techniques.
- Monitor and support TAs as they develop new questioning skills. Provide guidance, mentoring and opportunities to practise.
- Encourage TAs to become reflective practitioners and develop strategies in partnership with teachers.
- Include a review of TAs' questioning skills in their annual performance appraisal.

Supporting and developing pupils' independent learning skills

A job of any school and teacher is to develop the skills pupils need to thrive in school and beyond. Nurturing the development of 'soft skills' such as confidence, motivation and positive dispositions towards learning and attempting new things – in other words, learning to be independent and self-reliant – are all important for lifelong learning. Many schools profess to do just this, but to what extent do TAs share and support this goal in your school?

Much research, including our own and that led by Michael Giangreco in the USA, has revealed the unintentional, but nonetheless, damaging effects of pupil dependency on TA support. The DISS project and MAST study showed TAs can spoon-feed answers to pupils and that pupils can become quite used to TAs doing work for them. At worst, some pupils have effectively 'outsourced' their learning to a TA, such is their reliance on having someone available to complete work for them. It is worth bearing in mind these pupils tend to be the ones most in need of developing a stronger sense of themselves as capable and empowered learners. With the best of intentions, TAs can provide a form of support that protects pupils from their vulnerabilities, but there are serious long-term effects of such self-sustaining arrangements that have become embedded over time. Pupils receiving this type of support can grow ever less willing and ever less able to engage in learning tasks, because they lack the necessary underlying skills to face challenges with confidence.

More and more schools recognise the fundamental need for TAs to be included in the drive to enhance pupils' capacity to work independently; their interactions with pupils must serve this aim, rather than work against it. Schools in the EDTA project capitalised on the reality that TAs were well placed to be able to do this, in terms of having regular, sustained and active interactions with pupils. What needed to change was TAs' language.

Improving TAs' questioning skills will help you to develop pupils' thinking skills, but you should also develop complementary models of talk that help pupils to become independent learners. Such forms of TA talk are particularly useful for TAs deployed to lead classes. As pupils have to be more self-reliant in such situations, it is important they have the skills for taking greater ownership for their learning in the absence of the teacher. Again, you will need to raise awareness of the importance of developing pupils' independent learning skills, provide TAs with models of good practice and help them to hone these skills.

Raising awareness

In much the same way as we justified the necessity to develop TAs' questioning skills, school leaders must draw attention to the need for TAs to play a key role in fostering pupil independence. You should make this issue the subject of a meeting or training session for teachers and TAs. Discussion should emphasise the importance of developing resourceful, lifelong learners, both in terms of the benefits to the individuals themselves and to society in general.

Your school may run an initiative or programme, such as *Building Learning Power* or *Enquiring Minds*, which focuses on the development of transferable 'habits of mind' (or 'capabilities', 'competences', 'attributes' or 'dispositions', as they are variously known). If TAs are not familiar with the aims of the programme, you may be missing an opportunity to support the development of pupil independence.

Case study

Including TAs in wider school learning initiatives

One secondary school ran an initiative called *Building Learning Power*. BLP is a programme aimed at creating a culture of teaching and learning that systematically cultivates habits and attitudes to enable pupils to face difficulty and uncertainty calmly, confidently and creatively. At the start of the EDTA project, it was discovered that TAs were somewhat detached from the aims and teaching techniques used by BLP practitioners. The school held training for TAs and teachers encouraged and supported TAs to use and develop these skills in their interactions with pupils.

If the drive to improve pupil independence is backed up by the clear commitment and involvement of SLT, then TAs, along with all the teaching staff, will realise the importance the school is attaching to it. If robust linkages can be made between improved grades and the ability to learn independently, this will increase commitment.

If you are a teacher, you will no doubt by now be aware of how your decisions about TA deployment in the classroom can directly affect pupils' independence (see Chapter 4). Routinely deploying TAs to work with the same (often lower-attaining) pupils makes your expectations of such pupils clear: they are not capable of independent learning, so must be propped up by an adult. Inevitably, the pupil subconsciously believes this to be true and soon becomes dependent on the TA. The ramifications of this arrangement can be seen in the worst cases described in the MAST study (Webster and Blatchford 2014). Deploying TAs in alternative ways (e.g. strategic withdrawal of support at appropriate moments) emphasises the value of, and creates the conditions for, pupils thinking and acting for themselves.

Developing models of good practice

We have found many TAs have never before been given permission to depart from the default practices into which our research suggests many have settled. As you develop models of effective practice, you will need to instil a new culture that sets TAs free from the patterns of thought and action underpinning less effective practice.

A good example of this is 'stereo teaching'. This is the term we use to describe the effect of how intermittent talk from TAs to pupils during the teacher's whole-class input can effectively separate pupils from the teacher. The supported pupil hears two adult voices, rather than one, both very often saying the same thing – hence the stereo effect (for more, see Blatchford et al. 2012b).

TAs often talk when they do not need to. If they are listening to the teacher teach, and have not said anything for several minutes, their sense of needing to do something builds. We think this is an expression of how, in the absence of clarity over the role and purpose of effective support, TAs feel the need to justify their presence in the classroom. TAs say or do something – anything! – when in fact it is at times better for the pupils they support if they suppress this urge.

Similarly, TAs often describe a sense in which teachers judge their effectiveness in a lesson in terms of the quantity and/or quality of work produced by the pupils they support. This often leads TAs to take on too much of the task, spoon-feed answers and reduce the opportunity for pupils to think and work independently.

In both cases, TAs feel compelled to act in the interests of the pupils they are supporting. However, in these particular circumstances, greater educational benefits are likely to flow if they *do nothing*. This is counterintuitive, of course, but the evidence from the DISS project is clear on the effects of these types of TA-to-pupil interaction.

TAs need to be freed from this behaviour. They need to know it is acceptable for them to deprioritise task completion in favour of enabling more beneficial learning experiences. School leaders and teachers need to make it clear to TAs that it is preferable they act in ways that enable pupils to attempt tasks independently, rather than ensure there is some tangible outcome that can be shown to the teacher at the end of the lesson. It is better that a pupil completes three or four sums and genuinely understands the methods of calculation, than to produce a completed worksheet of correct answers, supplied by the TA, and learns nothing about the process by which they were derived. TAs generally act with the best of intentions, but this 'snow-plough' effect – removing the challenges and clearing a straight path to the solution – should concern all practitioners.

It is important to develop models of good practice. An initial step is to identify existing good practice and formally share this with TAs. As we have already mentioned, good teachers know the strategies and techniques for promoting pupil independence, but such knowledge needs to be made explicit for TAs.

Directing TAs' attention to forms of speech used by teachers to promote independence is another way of making tacit knowledge visible. In much the same way as we have described for developing effective questioning skills, teachers could model techniques in their interactions with pupils. TAs' observations can form the basis of a follow-up discussion to understand and refine their practice.

Knowing what to do when you do not know what to do

The essence of developing pupils' independent thinking skills is to inculcate a particular habit of mind, perhaps summed up best by paraphrasing Jean Piaget's definition of intelligence: knowing what to do when you do not know what to do. The role of TAs with pedagogical responsibilities should be to help pupils to help themselves, consistent with the 'guide on the side' view of teaching. While teachers have the primary responsibility for equipping pupils with the tools to think through ways in which to tackle new problems, TAs can assist by prompting pupils of certain steps to take to help them achieve this.

There is real value in developing forms of TA talk that serve this particular form of pedagogy, as they tend not to require specific subject knowledge. These skills are transferable between multiple contexts. Whether a pupil is stuck in history, mathematics, French or textiles, the formula for working through a problem is roughly the same: reflect on one's existing knowledge; draw on one's experience; look for clues in the current situation; and use other resources and tools to find an answer.

The role of the TA in such circumstances is to help pupils internalise and practise these valuable skills of self-sufficiency. Schools and teachers can work through examples of what this type of talk looks like and the particular questions or phrases appropriate at certain moments. These forms of talk have much in common with higher-order questions. Exemplar questions and phrases could be collected and collated to produce resources for TAs to use. Examples we have heard TAs use include:

- What is your plan?
- How can you find out about ...?
- What do you notice about ...?
- What do you know already that could help you?
- What happened when you got stuck before?
- How can you use what you learned last week to help you here?
- What can you use to help with this?
- Who else could help you?
- What would help you avoid distractions?
- What could you teach me about ...?

Note the subject of each question is the pupil. It is important to keep the responsibility for the learning and the doing with the pupil. TAs should avoid using 'us' or 'we' when asking questions; for example: 'How can *we* find out about ...?'

Some of the teachers in the EDTA project explored the use of pupil-led approaches to promote independent skills. Some introduced self-help strategies for which there was a clear logic: in order to develop the skills for independent thinking, pupils need to *be* independent, not have recourse to adult support. Other teachers used peer tutoring and peer supports. Both models have the effect of moving away from the tendency for adults to be pupils' first resort for assistance.

Case studies

Pupil self-help strategies 1

One primary school introduced classroom rules for independent learning. When stuck, pupils were expected to work through a sequence of strategies for tackling problems: re-read the question, ask a friend for help (but not the answer!); look for a resource that might help; *then* ask an adult for help.

Pupil self-help strategies 2

Teachers developed a self-help charter. The aim was to provide strategies for pupils to be more self-reliant and reduce instances of asking adults in the classroom for help straight away. The charter was moderated by senior leaders, then trialled.

Pupils were expected to try three different strategies before they asked the teacher or TA for help. Observations showed the trial was successful. Following some further tweaks, the charter was finalised and launched across the whole school. Copies of the charter were posted in each classroom and in printed pupils' diaries.

Having also trained TAs in methods of effective questioning, pupils were given opportunities to practise independence. Teachers ensured pupils had regular time in lessons to work without adult support, and reinforce the use of the self-help charter.

Encouraging pupils to think

One primary school TA was encouraged to turn pupil requests for assistance towards the rest of the group, thereby prioritising peer support over adult support. She also reflected questions back to pupils, in order to stimulate their own thinking. This practice also ensured that pupils retained the responsibility for their own learning.

Embedding and sustaining practice

As with developing effective questioning skills, it will take time for TAs to adopt the forms of talk aimed at promoting independent thinking skills and gain the confidence to make judgements about when to withdraw from pupils and when to return. TAs also need help and support to change ingrained habits. Some TAs have a controlling and intrusive manner, so acting in a more 'hands off', facilitative way will require training, guidance and plenty of opportunities to practise.

New ways of working that encourage pupils to become independent learners may challenge teachers, as well as TAs. School leaders should allow all staff time to adjust to the new practices and support them as they change their professional routines and relationships. It will be worthwhile. The approaches we have outlined should, in time, provide you with a much more effective TA workforce, contributing to, rather than undermining, efforts to develop confident and independent lifelong learners.

Key recommendations on supporting and developing pupils' independent learning skills

- Whole-school initiatives to develop pupils' independent learning skills must include an appropriate role for TAs.
- Instil a culture that sets TAs free from unhelpful patterns of thought driving less effective types of talk.
- Develop forms of talk that help pupils to know what to do when they do not know what to do.
- Ensure teachers explicitly model key techniques so TAs' practice is consistent with that of teachers.
- Produce resources with exemplars of question stems and effective prompts.
- Consider the use of pupil-led strategies (self-help and peer supports) as an alternative to adult support, and ensure pupils retain responsibility for their own learning.
- Allow time for new practices to bed in and take effect.
- Monitor and support TAs as they develop new skills and interaction techniques. Provide guidance, mentoring and opportunities to practice.

Developing TA-to-pupil talk

The interactions adults have with pupils and the language they use have long been recognised as playing an important role in pupil learning. Of course, there are other aspects of instructional talk that fall outside the two dimensions we have concentrated here, and there are inevitably different views on what constitutes effective teaching. However, it is possible to identify a number of common features from research (see Rubie-Davies et al. 2010):

- Effective teachers spend time orientating pupils to lessons and making links to prior learning.
- New concepts are introduced by providing high levels of instructional talk and checking pupils' understanding; effective teachers ask far more questions that require pupils to reason and engage in higher-level thinking.
- Effective teachers frequently provide pupils with feedback about their learning and encourage them to participate.
- For talk to actively promote pupil learning and conceptual understanding, effective teachers clearly articulate concepts and ideas, and skilfully scaffold pupil learning.

A consideration of this list makes it clear just how skilful teaching is, and how challenging it is for TAs when they are assigned a pedagogical role. It seems fair to say that in many schools TAs have taken on a frontline instructional role, but schools have not really considered the nature of the talk that takes place.

This presents a dilemma: is it realistic to expect TAs to talk to pupils in the same way as teachers, informed by the same degree of training in subject and instructional knowledge? Can we really expect TAs to use talk in service of the kinds of effective teaching summarised above? Or can we train TAs for a role that takes on some of the characteristics of effective teaching, and which is properly calibrated to realistic expectations?

Could in fact, a well thought through model of TA-to-pupil talk, which makes a distinct contribution to learning, be a 'ground-up' way of rethinking the role and purpose of TAs?

TAs as scaffolders of learning

Since TAs frequently work with small groups and individuals, they are in the unique position of being able to constantly monitor the step-by-step progress pupils make towards achieving learning goals. From this vantage point, TAs can provide immediate feedback and give targeted support with the parts of tasks pupils find difficult. This is called *scaffolding*, and it is the key to ensuring pupils become able to work more independently.

Effective scaffolding ensures pupils are fully engaged in the task and that the potential for learning is maximised. It also ensures that, over time, pupils develop the capability to carry out tasks without support and have the confidence in themselves to attempt more challenging tasks. Scaffolding is a quite ubiquitous phrase in schools, but the practice it is used to describe is often some distance from the very specific set of skills we have in mind. For us, scaffolding involves:

- Recognising a task as a series of smaller learning goals.
- Carefully observing the progress pupils make as they complete each part of the task.
- Only intervening if a pupil has not been able to overcome a difficulty independently (i.e. giving them time to try by themselves first).
- Giving specific help or feedback when a pupil needs help with part of a task.
- Providing the minimal amount of help pupils need to achieve.

The scaffolding process encourages pupils to think of strategies they can use to solve problems for themselves; in other words, to know what to do when they do not know what to do. The refrain that underpins good scaffolding is the notion of providing the *least* amount of help during each interaction. This is in stark contrast to what was found in the DISS project, where TAs would correct and give answers with little or no prompting from pupils; in other words, the *most* amount of help.

Scaffolding is the key to providing a quality learning experience, and when carried out correctly, it leads to not only greater independence, but also to an improved ability to cope with learning challenges and setbacks (often referred to as 'resilience'). Long-term effects extend to pupils being more positively disposed to accepting failure as an inevitable and healthy part of learning, and developing a deeper engagement in, and appreciation of, learning for learning's sake.

On the basis of evidence from recent studies (Radford et al. 2014; Radford et al. 2015) and our on-going work with schools (including the MITA programme) we have found TAs can be highly effective when given a good understanding of the importance of scaffolding and a clear role as the scaffolder of pupils' learning.

Consistent with, but greatly expanding on, what we have covered in this chapter, our accompanying handbook for TAs – *The Teaching Assistant's Guide To Effective Interaction: How to Maximise Your Impact* (Bosanquet, Radford and Webster 2016) – focuses on the transformative power of scaffolding in the learning process. It contains lots of practical strategies, techniques and reflective activities for TAs to try, which support whole-school training and development.

School leaders seeking to improve TA-to-pupil interactions would do well to read it alongside this book in order to obtain the fullest expression of how our extensive research has led to the comprehensive guidance set out in the two books.

TAs and collaborative group-work

In the DISS project we were struck by the way TAs did not always appreciate the tacit intentions behind group-work and how their involvement in group-work could work against the overarching aims of independent learning. To be fair, research conducted in the Social Pedagogic Research into Group-work (SPRinG) project, co-directed by Peter Blatchford, found teachers themselves did not always see the benefits of collaborative activities; that is, pupils working *as* a group, rather than in a group. They seemed to have difficulty in setting up good quality group-work experiences.

We have found working effectively with groups requires a rethink from the usual way adults work with pupils: a move away from an obviously interactive role to something akin to the 'guide on the side' role already referred to. One of the main benefits of group-work is it can allow pupils to learn from each other: through the exchange of ideas; having to justify and explain points of view; developing new explanations; and so on. We found in the SPRinG project that setting up quality group-work required careful support from teachers, thoughtful preparation of the classroom and the tasks, and specific training and guidance for pupils in how to work collaboratively; for example, setting ground rules and valuing one another's contributions.

Given many teachers tell us that they have difficulties with group-work, it is not surprising that TAs do too. In particular, we have found that the adult support approach recommended for collaborative group-work, which deliberately allows pupils greater control over their learning, requires a different mindset. TAs, as we have discussed, tend to feel obliged to regularly interact with pupils and this cuts across peer interactions. In doing so, TAs adversely affect the development of independent learning skills by limiting the opportunities for pupils to talk and discuss. Being the 'guide on the side' requires TAs to resist the compulsion to intervene, and instead, steer and coax gently from the sidelines.

The chapter on TAs and group-work in *The Teaching Assistant's Guide...* describes how TAs can support pupils when working as groups on collaborative tasks. For more on this topic, readers may also like to refer to *Promoting Effective Group Work in the Primary Classroom: A Handbook for Teachers and Practitioners*, by Baines et al. (2008).

Summary

Many school leaders and teachers do not need to be convinced that effective interactions are at the heart of learning. Given the evidence shows TAs' talk to pupils works against achieving both short-term and long-term educational aims, it is essential that school leaders take the issue of improving TA–pupil interactions seriously. Schools that participated in the EDTA project and the MITA programme, together with many others that have acted on the guidance in this book, have put in place in-house training and support to transform the nature, quality and purpose of TAs' talk. Schools that have taken these steps report that TAs' interactions:

- Have a greater focus on learning – *not* task completion.
- Tend far less towards correction.
- Allow more space for pupils to think and respond.
- Have a better balance of open-ended and close-ended questions.
- Are timed and paced to allow pupils space to think and work independently.

Chapter 6

The preparedness of TAs

Introduction

How well prepared are your newly qualified teachers (NQTs)? Are they adequately prepared to teach their specialist subjects, or in the case of primary school NQTs, *all* subjects? In particular, how well has their training prepared them to meet the learning needs of pupils with SEN, and those who underperform academically? What about the level of their day-to-day preparation? Are you aware of how well these NQTs are prepared for each day's lessons? Are you confident their lesson plans are clear, detailed and matched to the learning needs of their pupils?

Now replace the references to 'NQTs' in the questions above with 'teaching assistants' and ask yourself the same questions again.

Many school leaders we meet *think* they know the answers, but when asked *how* they know, their answers are less convincing. If you do not deploy TAs to teach your pupils – that is, they are confined to non-pedagogical roles – then these questions are not so relevant. But as you will be aware (and as the DISS project showed), most TAs spend more time teaching pupils than doing anything else. Therefore, the chances are these questions are very relevant to the situation in your school and must be addressed as part of your wider thinking about reforming the TA role.

The focus of this chapter is preparedness, which is the third of the three main components of the Wider Pedagogical Role model. As we saw in the Introduction, there are two aspects of TA preparedness:

1   TAs' overall preparation for their role.
2   TAs' day-to-day preparation for supporting particular subjects, lessons, tasks and pupils.

The findings from the DISS project concerning TA preparation (see Chapter 1) are a cause for concern. It is essential, therefore, both aspects of preparedness are reviewed and modified to ensure TAs are better prepared for the work school leaders and teachers ask them to do.

In Chapter 4, we stated that decisions about deployment provide the starting point from which all other decisions about TAs flow. Having established what roles you want TAs to perform and how they should be deployed and interact with pupils, you will need to consider the appropriate forms of preparation needed for them to succeed. In this chapter, we consider the decision-making required concerning aspects of preparation both at the school level and, in sections headed 'Teacher-level decisions', at the classroom level.

It should be said that although improving TAs' preparedness has inevitable consequences for teachers' preparedness (that is, how well they are able to work with and manage TAs), the purpose of this chapter is to offer guidance on how to improve the preparedness of TAs, rather than teachers. The DISS project showed the issue of working with TAs has not been given enough attention in initial teacher education (ITE), and the preparedness of teachers is therefore as important as that of TAs. Our view is that ITE providers must address this deficit more fully, but clearly this matter is beyond the scope of this book. For school leaders, the key message is this: if you take seriously the need for teachers to plan, manage and evaluate the work of TAs successfully, you need to provide teachers with further training opportunities to help them achieve this. We highlight this throughout this chapter where relevant.

Some important questions to ask about teachers' training

- In your judgement, have your teachers been adequately prepared to work with and organise the TAs and other adults that work regularly in their classrooms?
- Have your teachers been adequately trained to share or delegate teaching with TAs?
- Do you know what training your teachers have had in order to support the needs of pupils with SEN?

The results of your audit will inform decisions about how to deploy TAs in appropriate roles. Once this has been decided, you will need to think about how you train TAs for these roles and put in place processes and systems to support their day-to-day preparation. Broadly put, you will need to consider the types of preparation required for TAs in pedagogical roles and non-pedagogical roles.

Preparedness for TAs with non-pedagogical roles

Supporting teachers

Training

As we have previously mentioned, perhaps the most extreme expression of a non-pedagogical TA role is one in which TAs do not routinely interact with pupils. If you have chosen to create roles for TAs that help teachers with their routine clerical tasks, it may be necessary to offer forms of training. Some tasks, like data entry, will require using specific software. In some secondary schools, TAs may take on invigilation, so they will need to be fully conversant with the protocols of overseeing examinations.

In this book we have explored the potential for TAs to have a behaviour management role in classrooms, which again would require targeted training in specific techniques, such as de-escalation, and which have a consistent fit with your school's behaviour policy.

Day-to-day preparation

Daily preparation for TAs in non-pedagogical roles is unlikely to require regular meetings between teachers and TAs. Most of what needs to be communicated can be done in fairly *ad hoc* ways or through written notes. For example, we are aware of some teachers who keep a 'jobs book' in which they maintain a list of administrative tasks TAs can do during quieter moments.

In terms of the day-to-day preparation for TAs with a behaviour monitoring role, there will be a need for teachers and TAs to share information at the start and end of lessons. This might include, for example, whether any pupils have had a difficult morning or experienced trouble at home the night before, and are therefore more likely to be volatile or fractious during the lesson. The teacher will mostly be aware of the behaviour incidents that will need to be followed up after a lesson, should any occur. This, therefore, reduces the need for TA feedback after the lesson. Nonetheless, TAs should be encouraged to briefly feed back any relevant information of which the teacher may not be aware before they leave the classroom.

Supporting pupils' physical and emotional needs

Training

TAs who support pupils with physical/mobility, visual or hearing impairments are very likely to have already had particular training in appropriate techniques, such as handling or sign language. Following your review of TA roles, any TA deployed in such a role who has not had training will need to be trained, and there may be a need for some to update their training.

As we noted in Chapter 4, TAs are often well positioned to support pupils' emotional needs. TAs often have the appropriate characteristics (e.g. warmth and attentiveness) required for nurturing roles. However, these cannot be considered sufficient qualifications for supporting pupils' emotional development, especially where this is likely to be quite complex, as in the case of those who have experienced trauma in early childhood. You will need to ensure TAs are properly trained and qualified to take on nurturing or counselling-type roles. Programmes delivered by ELSAs to support pupil wellbeing, for example, train TAs to use basic counselling techniques (e.g. active listening and problem clarification) to guide conversations. It is advisable that anyone undertaking higher-level counselling work receives appropriate supervision from a suitably qualified person. ELSAs, for example, receive regular professional supervision from an educational psychologist.

Day-to-day preparation

There are a number of ways in which TAs who support pupils with physical needs will need to be prepared in similar ways to TAs in pedagogical roles (more of which later). They may need access to teachers' lesson resources in advance in order to make specific modifications, for example, making enlarged photocopies of worksheets for visually impaired pupils. Any prior knowledge of lesson content will help TAs to prepare in advance; for example, how they will convey particular information or concepts to hearing impaired pupils via sign language.

As with the daily preparation for TAs in behaviour monitoring roles, it will be necessary for TAs who support pupils with physical needs to share some information with teachers at the start and end of the lesson, regarding, for example, the organisation of the lesson and the classroom; will the TA need to make any particular modifications in order to ensure the pupil can access the lesson? For pupils with emotional needs, TAs can once again inform teachers at the start of the lesson of any factors that may affect their engagement and behaviour during the lesson. In both cases, feedback from TAs at the end of the lesson will be necessary to inform future lesson planning.

It is for you and your SLT to make the forms of day-to-day preparation and feedback described above obligatory throughout the school. This expectation can be written into your school policy on TA deployment. Routine feedback will enable teachers to become more informed about how pupils respond to their lessons and their teaching style, and allow them to reflect meaningfully on their practice.

Key recommendations on preparing TAs for non-pedagogical roles

- Ensure TAs with behaviour management roles receive thorough training in classroom and pupil management techniques. Make sure use of these techniques is consistently applied across the school.
- TAs who support pupils' physical and social development should receive formal training and hold the necessary qualifications to perform these roles.
- Ensure teachers brief TAs at the start of lessons and that there are mechanisms for obtaining feedback.
- Identify a set of particular tasks (e.g. modifying resources) TAs can do to help teachers prepare for meeting the needs of pupils with physical or sensory needs in classrooms.

Preparedness for TAs with pedagogical roles

> There is an assumption that you should just know. You're to come into a classroom, you listen to the 20 minutes of teaching, and from that – if you didn't know, you should know now. And then you're to feed it to the children. It's scary.
>
> (Primary TA)

The comment above was one of the most powerful to emerge from the interviews we conducted as part of the EDTA project. It sums up the problem school leaders must seek to resolve in relation to preparing TAs adequately for pedagogical roles. The primary school TA encapsulates the difficulty of 'going into lessons blind' and the implications for learning of having to tune into the teachers' whole-class input in order to get vital information, which in turn must be differentiated on the hoof, so the pupils that struggle most to access learning can make sense of the curriculum. Little wonder the TA describes this challenge as 'scary'.

From hereon in, we set out strategies that mitigate the problems of going into lessons blind and, moreover, seek to avoid this situation in the first place. We deal principally with school-level issues of training and organising preparation time, but there are specific, more detailed, issues concerning lesson planning and feedback that we cover at the classroom-level, in the sections headed 'Teacher-level decisions'.

Training

The outcome of your school staff audit will show the range of qualifications and skills held by your TAs and highlight any gaps in training you need to fill. In light of this process, you should consider training to raise the quality of TAs' contributions to pupils' learning and academic progress for those you plan to deploy in pedagogical roles.

Seek to implement a comprehensive and coherent whole-school strategy to address these gaps. As we have made clear, taking steps to change TAs' levels of preparedness should not precede efforts to address the training needs of teachers. In other words, you must avoid skilling-up TAs as a proxy for addressing gaps in teachers' pedagogical knowledge and skills, especially when it comes to meeting the needs of lower-attaining pupils and those with SEN.

Some training can be aimed at both groups of staff, while other courses, sessions and interventions can be targeted at one group, or even at individuals. So even though this chapter does not expressly deal with how you might meet the training needs of teachers, there may be some things you develop for TAs that teachers may benefit from too.

Developing TAs' subject and pedagogical knowledge

Few would argue subject knowledge and understanding are fundamental to effective teaching. Therefore, any deficit in the TAs' subject knowledge must be met with action of some kind. Indeed, when arriving at a judgment on the effectiveness of teaching, learning and assessment, Ofsted inspectors evaluate the extent to which TAs 'have relevant subject knowledge that is detailed and communicated well to pupils' (Ofsted 2015).

For TAs with a pedagogical role, quality training in teaching will also be necessary, so they are better equipped to convey their knowledge to pupils. The comment below from one of the TAs involved in the EDTA project evokes the dangers of the 'training trap' mentioned in Chapter 4:

> I don't know whether they [SLT] think, because we did insets on certain things, and they may cover that subject for half a morning, that's sufficient enough – which it clearly isn't. Maybe that's what they think. But me personally, I don't think it's enough. If you want me to do interventions, send me on a course. It's as simple as that.
>
> (Primary TA)

The need for TAs to have pedagogical skills has, historically speaking, been neglected. The DISS project made clear the effects of untested assumptions about how easily TAs would be able to take on roles more appropriately within the realm of teachers. Teaching is a highly skilled process and it is unfair to TAs, and to pupils especially, to expect TAs to develop these skills without specific preparation.

TAs will always have a supplemental role and so their subject and pedagogical knowledge will be particular and not the same as that of teachers. Our view is that school leaders need to appropriately calibrate TAs' teaching role relative to that of the teacher and ensure there is no formal responsibility for outcomes attached to what TAs do. We think a good expression of the type of role that fits this description is the scaffolding role we introduced at the end of the previous chapter.

When schools adopt this approach, much of what TAs require in terms of developing both their subject and pedagogical knowledge can be achieved through in-house training. You could, for example, introduce regular informal 'mini-tutorials' for TAs, where teachers can brief them on topic information or technical processes (e.g. performing more complex mathematical operations). This could extend to 'question and answer' sessions where TAs meet with subject specialists to get guidance and advice on concepts and processes. Teachers can use these sessions to keep informed of TAs' working knowledge and to check their understanding of the syllabus and instructional techniques.

Schools we have worked with, including those in the EDTA project, have successfully delivered in-house training to improve TAs' subject knowledge and pedagogical skills. They draw on the expertise of teachers and TAs to share good practice and to provide guidance and support through targeted training, peer observations and feedback, all of which have been found to be both valuable and cost-effective.

Case studies

Boosting TAs' basic skills 1

The school decided that qualifications to at least Level Two in literacy and numeracy (i.e. equivalent to a GCSE pass) would be a prerequisite for all new TA appointments, with posts advertised as such. To address the fact that some existing TAs did not have these Level Two qualifications (as revealed via an audit of TAs' skills and qualifications), SLT arranged for external tutors to come into school to help these TAs achieve these qualifications. TAs, some of who felt they had been failed by the school system, appreciated this 'second chance' to obtain these vital qualifications.

Boosting TAs' basic skills 2

Some TAs were unconfident using ICT equipment, so the school arranged sessions to boost their skills and confidence with technology; iPad training, for example, helped TAs to download apps to use with groups. TAs' confidence with ICT improved, and extra training sessions were held for those who continued to struggle.

Watching and discussing a video of an experienced and effective TA in action

Teachers and TAs from one school watched a video recording of a TA colleague working with a group of pupils in a science lesson. This provided a useful springboard for a discussion about effective TA practice, which included how the TA used her time in the session and the instructional techniques she used.

Case study

The Lesson Study approach

Lesson Study is a peer observation technique with origins in Japanese education. Adapted for the purposes of developing teaching practice among teacher–TA teams, staff in one three-form entry primary school worked collaboratively in small groups to discuss learning goals and plan a 'research lesson', which members of the group either delivered or observed. They then discussed and revised for a second iteration, with observers and deliverers swapping roles. The outcomes (e.g. what went well, not so well, etc.) were later shared with all school staff.

The three teachers and three TAs in each year group planned and delivered a research lesson. Importantly, colleagues did not judge or grade one another's performance in the lesson. Instead, the focus was on groups or specific pupils and their learning journey through the lesson. The deputy headteacher said: 'As they have all planned the lesson together, it is much easier to discuss where things maybe have not worked. TAs have found it very useful to observe other colleagues and learn from each other's practice.'

Training for TAs in how to manage interactions with pupils, how to select and use effective strategies for learning and how to help pupils when they are stuck is crucial, but has been generally lacking in any formal and consistent way. It is not enough to expect TAs to absorb these skills by simply sitting in the classroom and watching the teacher teach.

We have already drawn attention to the amount of time TAs spend in a passive role, listening to teachers deliver their input to the class, but teachers in the EDTA project found these moments can be valuable training opportunities. Before the lesson, teachers directed TAs' attention to specific techniques they modelled in their whole-class input, and which they wanted TAs to use when they supported a group later in the lesson.

Of course, it might not be possible or practical to meet all training needs for TAs through in-house training. External training may be necessary, particularly in preparing TAs to support and interact with pupils with particular types of SEN or to deliver particular curriculum interventions. Continuing professional development (CPD) that leads to qualifications and accreditation should be available and will formalise the acquisition of new skills, as well as enhancing TAs' confidence and self-image.

School leaders might wish to consider delivering training for TAs and teachers on effective classroom talk using this book's sister publication, *The Teaching Assistant's Guide to Effective Interaction* (Bosanquet, Radford and Webster 2016).

Training for TAs who lead classes

In Chapter 4, we explored the role of TAs leading classes as part of school arrangements to release teachers for PPA time and/or to cover short-term teacher absence. If you choose to deploy TAs to lead classes you need to ensure they have the skills and training to succeed. Again, a programme of in-house training should be developed to ensure TAs are given quality training from experienced teachers in classroom management skills. The role and the training will be framed by the expectations set out in the school policy on the appropriate use of TAs to work in place of teachers. Monitoring and mentoring should also feature as crucial elements of the training programme, so TAs are supported in the early stages of their role.

Key recommendations for preparing TAs with pedagogical roles

- Consider cost-effective in-house approaches to developing TAs' subject and pedagogical knowledge (e.g. mini-tutorials, observations), so they are more able to promote thinking and learning through their interactions with pupils.
- Ensure TAs that lead classes receive training in classroom management and are supported by wider school systems.

Induction and performance review

Induction

We have heard anecdotally of TAs receiving highly questionable forms of induction consisting of little more than reading pupils' individual educational plans and Statements of SEN, or looking through resources packs and material from intervention programmes. While in no way commendable, worse than this is no induction at all, which we have found is a common experience amongst TAs we have met. Similarly, teachers have told us that even where they have received some form of induction, it rarely included anything substantive on what the school expected from them in terms of TA deployment.

Our view is that all newly appointed TAs and teachers (including trainees) should receive a full induction into the school's expectations and practices relating to the work of TAs.

The school policy on TA deployment is a useful vehicle for structuring induction and training around what the school expects from new teachers, and what new TAs can expect from teachers, in terms of being adequately prepared and deployed for pedagogical tasks.

Valuable models of school induction we have encountered include opportunities for new TAs to shadow experienced and effective TAs. If this is extended to new teachers as well, this form of shadowing will help new staff to have a better understanding of what the policy means in practice. Furthermore, through lesson observations, new appointees will be exposed to what the school regards as exemplary teacher–TA collaboration in lessons. Some schools in the EDTA project were seeking to use video recordings of TAs in action as part of their induction training. New staff could sit in on teacher–TA planning and feedback meetings to see how lesson plans are used and shared, once again providing the opportunity for them to get familiar with the kinds of practice the school will expect them to adopt.

Introduction to the school policy, shadowing TAs and observing teacher–TA meetings and lessons should be the focus of on-going discussion to ensure the intended outcomes have been achieved. The significant points of what it means for TAs to be properly prepared need to understood and 'made real' if you are to achieve consistent school-wide practice.

New teachers and TAs should be observed in the early stages of their appointment in order to get feedback on their performance and guidance for further development. Such comments on the performance of their roles can also be used to reassure them and you that the school's TA policy is being used correctly and effectively. It can also reveal aspects that have been overlooked or misunderstood. Feedback depends on some form of monitoring of teachers' and TAs' preparation, which should be led by the SLT.

Performance review and audit cycle

Of course, monitoring the work of new staff is not a one-off activity. As new teachers and TAs become established members of your workforce, they will become part of the annual performance review process. Their performance, in terms of how they uphold or are supported by the school's policy on TAs, should form part of your overall evaluation of their performance. In particular, this will have greater implications for teachers than for TAs, as it is teachers' decision-making that is under scrutiny; with TAs' effectiveness being determined by these decisions.

In Chapter 2, we suggested school leaders use the whole-school audit to review the implementation of new models of TA deployment, preparation and practice. Indeed, the audit could be used annually (maybe not in full, but at least components of it) to help you update your records on TAs' qualifications and training. A regular audit cycle is intended to maintain the identification of training needs, and SLT should make provision for the necessary updating of staffs' knowledge and skills.

Case study

Coaching for TAs

TA training was made a high priority for all staff. Members of the SLT took on a coaching role. They observed TAs at least once each half term and provided constructive feedback. Coaches modelled good practice and discussed approaches used.

There were many misconceptions about what constituted good practice and these were addressed in the observations and coaching. SLT noted that organising observations and feeding back to TAs was a large undertaking and it took time. But subsequent observations and feedback from TAs found that new techniques and strategies were being adopted and implemented. TAs also reported feeling more confident when supporting groups. Overall, the effort to introduce the coaching was paying dividends.

Key recommendations on induction and performance review

- Introduce a formal programme of induction for new teachers and TAs on TA deployment, structured around the school's policy on TAs.
- Induction training could include the opportunity to shadow an experienced, effective TA.
- Ensure new teachers and TAs receive support and guidance in the early stages of their appointment.
- Use the auditing tools to carry out an annual review of how the school policy is being implemented, and to identify and meet gaps in teachers' and TAs' knowledge and skills.

Day-to-day preparedness

The evidence is clear that TAs are generally under-prepared for the tasks teachers ask them to do daily, which is not surprising when you consider that three-quarters of teachers surveyed in the DISS project had no allocated time to meet with TAs. Our view is this situation must improve if schools are serious about TAs having a positive impact on learning outcomes.

Your audit will have revealed the picture in your school regarding the opportunities available for teachers and TAs to meet, plan, prepare and feedback, and the nature and quality of information that flows between them. It is very likely there will be echoes of the DISS project findings in your audit results. If this is the case, you will need to develop and implement a school-wide strategy to formalise the ways teachers and TAs communicate.

Many school leaders and teachers do not need to be convinced of the need to provide opportunities for teachers and TAs to prepare for lessons and to feedback afterwards. But for many, it is the capacity to create this time that is the real problem. Before we go any further, it is worth stating upfront we appreciate that for many school leaders, creating meeting time means extending TAs' hours of work, and thus has a financial implication. The current pressures on school funding are such that extending TAs' contracted hours to create meeting time with teachers before and/or after school may be considered a luxury, and for most, something that is not a spending priority.

However, school leaders *must* see the need for some form of liaison as central to making the best use of TAs. Without opportunities to meet and discuss lessons with teachers, all efforts to improve the contribution and value of your TA workforce will be undermined and potentially undone. As one secondary headteacher whose school participated in the MITA programme said: 'I started this process thinking I can't afford to create meeting time for teachers and TAs. But it wasn't long before I realised I can't afford *not* to create meeting time for teachers and TAs'.

Creating time for teachers and TAs to meet

Your audit will reveal the answers to three key questions that can help provide the starting point for reform:

1   How much time, if any, do your teachers and TAs have to meet?
2   If they have meeting time, is this used effectively to brief TAs on lessons and for teachers to receive quality feedback?
3   If they do not have time to meet, how do teachers communicate to TAs their lesson plans, lesson tasks and activities, expected learning outcomes *and* the role they need them to take in lessons?

If teachers and TAs in your school do not have timetabled sessions in which to meet (i.e. within their paid hours of work), you must change something to make such meetings part of the routine pattern of teacher–TA collaboration. We know from the DISS project results that TAs worked, on average, an additional three hours voluntarily each week, spending much of that time in discussion with teachers. Many headteachers we interviewed were aware of how this could easily be seen as exploitative, though few had sought to do anything about it as, like many other schools, they relied quite heavily on TAs' goodwill; without it, there would likely be no teacher–TA meetings at all.

Present arrangements, therefore, have to move away from the commonly found practice of using TAs' own unpaid time to hold planning and feedback meetings. If schools choose to use TAs to teach, then surely they must take steps to allow them to be adequately prepared for the work teachers ask them to do. Similarly, if pupils are taught by TAs away from the classroom, then feedback for teachers is even more essential for assessment and planning purposes. There is a clear need to formalise teacher–TA liaison time, so overall practice can improve in ways that make positive effects on pupil learning more likely.

Many school leaders and teachers we have spoken to maintain that in order to get best value from their TAs, they should spend every working moment with pupils. However, there is a strong case for using part of the TAs' time each week for planning and preparation, so that they can be more effective the rest of the time when supporting and interacting with pupils. If, for example, TAs lead interventions, consider the added value that would be derived from providing dedicated time for them to plan and prepare thoroughly for these sessions. As we have said already, the use of interventions should *at least* compensate for time spent away from the teacher. But this cannot happen by solely putting your faith in the quality of the intervention programme. If schools withdraw pupils from classes for TA-led interventions, every effort must be made to ensure TAs have opportunities to properly prepare in order to help them deliver sessions to maximum effect. This should be a 'non-negotiable' of using pull-out programmes, or else you are unlikely to see the accelerated progress they promise.

Creating the kind of time we are referring to is most effectively achieved by extending TAs' hours of work, and that of course, costs money. But as we have already mentioned, it was a deliberate part of the EDTA project design to encourage schools to think creatively and to come up with solutions within their existing resources. Some schools looked for spaces in the school day where teachers and TAs could meet, such as during assemblies or teachers' PPA time. Some schools, notably primaries, were already doing this prior to the project.

Some schools acknowledged that changing TAs' contracts and hours of work was necessary for a significant improvement of TAs' level of preparedness. One possibility is to retain the same number of contracted hours, but to shift the start and end times, allowing teachers to have a set time for meeting with TAs at the start or end of the school day. If you possibly can, increase TAs' hours specifically to provide time to meet teachers. Both options will send out a strong and clear message: you are serious about ensuring TAs are better prepared to teach pupils in your school, and serious about raising the esteem of the TA role.

The case studies below are drawn from schools we have worked with, including some from the EDTA project. They show how schools have addressed the problem of creating liaison time by deploying a mix of approaches, not all of which relied on extending TAs' working hours.

Case studies

Creating liaison time for TAs and teachers 1

'If TAs do not feel that teachers listen to them or value their feedback, they will provide weak feedback or no feedback.' This was the starting point for SLT, who restructured their support staff team around creating time for teachers and TAs to have meaningful dialogue. TAs' contracts were extended to allow half an hour meeting time before school every day. Each week, one of these slots was used for training, giving TAs an extra 20 hours CPD each year.

Creating liaison time for TAs and teachers 2

The poor communication between teachers and TAs was a cause of low morale among TAs. The school employed coaches to deliver PE lessons and to release teachers and TAs for one hour of dedicated PPA time a week. It was teachers' responsibility to ensure that TAs were clear on their role in lessons; the SLT set this as 'non-negotiable'.

A rota was used to allow the majority of teachers and TAs to be freed up to meet for 20 minutes during assembly on a Friday. During these sessions, teachers and TAs completed a weekly dialogue record. Ring-fencing liaison time in this way had the effect of allowing space for quality conversations, planning and preparation.

Creating liaison time for TAs and teachers 3

TAs' hours of work were extended in order to create time to meet at the start of the school day. There was a consultation with TAs on the new contracts as it was recognised that many had childcare commitments that they needed to address in order to accommodate the change to their working hours. A solution was found for all TAs, so from the start of the next school year, teachers and TAs had 15 minutes preparation time at the beginning of each school day to plan and discuss.

Creating liaison time for TAs and teachers 4

TAs' working hours were extended so that they could meet with teachers at the start and end of the day. But in order to ensure a continuity and efficiency of service, all TA positions were converted into full-time roles. Both teachers and TAs valued the time to meet, and the changes led to TAs having greater involvement in the planning process.

Creating liaison time for TAs and teachers 5

Rather than extend TAs' hours, one primary school brought the start and finish times of the TAs' days forward by 15 minutes to create guaranteed time for teachers and TAs to meet and discuss. SLT set the expectation that teachers must set out what the class were going to do each day and what roles they and the TA would take in lessons. This time also provided the opportunity for the TA to feed back anything from the previous day.

Both the teacher and the TA described this arrangement as 'invaluable'. This decision followed a trial in two classes. It had been so successful that the school had decided to change the working hours of all its TAs in the same way. The governing body approved and from the start of the following school year, all teachers and TAs had daily liaison time.

It is important for you and your SLT to actively monitor the teachers' actual use of any meeting time you create. Simply providing a space in the school day does not guarantee that teachers will know how to make best use of this precious time. At the outset, you should make your expectations known about how the time should be used, and ensure you monitor what is going on by making regular checks.

If TAs have a pedagogical role, using planning time to wash paint pots or do photocopying for the teacher does not represent the best use of time. You need to be clear how preparation time should be used effectively, and if necessary provide specific suggestions, guidelines or models to assist teachers. The broad intention of setting such time aside is to raise TAs' levels of preparedness, with the expectation this will improve their interactions with pupils (see Chapter 5) and, in turn, raise pupil attainment. This is the point that needs to be emphasised and reiterated.

It is worth noting the implication in the second case study below, that SLT also have to treat preparation time as sacrosanct and not deny its potential by withdrawing TAs at short notice for other duties.

Case studies

Using liaison time effectively 1

SLT were keen to ensure that newly created preparation time was used efficiently, so teachers used a structured lesson plan to frame discussions. It emerged that some conversations lacked focus, so training was put in place on effective communications to ensure the morning meetings were as effective as possible.

Using liaison time effectively 2

TAs had a dedicated timetabled slot each week, joining their class teacher for the last 30 minutes of their PPA time to share the following week's lesson plans and the role of TAs within lessons. Teachers were expected to provide clear expectations for the TA role, agreeing and clarifying roles and responsibilities around the principle that the teacher has the main teaching role.

SLT noted that the success of this relied on the teacher having prepared lessons in advance of the meeting and the TA being present (e.g. that the TA would not be deployed elsewhere at short notice).

Lesson planning

DEVELOPING A LESSON PLAN TEMPLATE

One way of formalising what you expect teachers to provide in terms of TA preparation is to develop a lesson plan template that specifically requires teachers to set out their instructions to TAs. The template should prompt teachers to give adequate thought to what TAs will do during lessons and what they need to know in order to do it effectively. The template should feature in your school policy on TAs, again acting as a reminder of how serious the school is about preparing TAs for teaching. It should be possible to set this template up in an electronic format, enabling documents to be shared and modified, so TAs can add comments and feedback.

TEACHER-LEVEL DECISIONS

By and large, we have found TAs acquire the knowledge they need for lessons by tuning into the teacher's delivery – just like the TA from the EDTA project in the earlier comment. Many teachers argue this is a form of preparation, but this is more like improvisation, and a misuse of valuable lesson time.

Although in this book we have suggested that the three-part lesson plan is a helpful way of framing TAs' roles in lessons, we are not implying this is the only, or best, way to structure teaching and learning. Indeed, for lessons that take a different format and are, say, light on whole-class input, teachers will need to use secure methods to bring TAs up to speed.

Making the best use of TAs requires teachers to think carefully about how they build the TA into their lessons and communicate this to them. As well as arming TAs with the requisite subject and pedagogical knowledge, teachers need to ensure they plan lessons with an awareness of what it is they specifically want TAs to do. Teachers must provide TAs with explicit roles and tasks. Merely listing the names of the pupils teachers want the TA to support, for instance, is not enough. Equally, writing the TA's initials alongside things on the lesson plan that are more relevant to teachers is not sufficient.

Teachers' overview of the curriculum, the scope and content of a unit of work, and the sequential development of concepts and understanding, all contribute to their understanding of a lesson plan. TAs tend not to have the same level of pedagogical awareness of the context in which a lesson plan is set. Furthermore, the same TA may not be present lesson-to-lesson. This is a particular issue in secondary schools; partly an artifact of the way the TA role is a part-time position in the majority of schools, and also how TAs tend to be spread across a wide range of subjects.

Teachers' lesson plans and whole-class delivery should make their intentions explicit and remove the need for the TAs to guess what was in their minds, assume they will pick up salient points, or interpret brief notes on plans. It is too easy to assume TAs have access to the implicit knowledge teachers hold as the skilled pedagogues. Teachers need to provide TAs with detailed and clear information about the tasks they assign to them: key concepts, facts and information to be taught; skills to be learned, applied, practised or extended; and the intended outcomes, in terms of products and learning. Think in terms of the lesson 'need to knows': the four or five critical things the TA will need to be aware of in order to make the best contribution to the lesson. A lesson plan template can provide focus and consistency (see above).

Teachers' plans could include questions and strategies for TAs to use when teaching individuals or groups. Be clear about how tasks can be sequenced and the time available in which to complete them.

Some tasks teachers deploy TAs to undertake may be less pedagogical in nature, but should be made clear nonetheless in their planning. For example, teachers in early years settings commonly use TAs to observe and record pupil performance or engagement during lessons for assessment purposes. This is a smart way to use TAs, as observation requires identifying and recording responses to interactions, and does not require making any intervention; though TAs must be trained in order to conduct observations reliably. TAs and early years support workers provide valuable data for teachers that they might otherwise miss in a busy classroom of 30 or more young children. This information is used to compile each pupil's learning journey and feeds into teachers' further task planning and assessment. If you work in a school with an early years setting, there is much to be learned about TA preparation and deployment that can be imported into classrooms much further up the school.

As we have stated, creating time for teachers and TAs to meet to plan and prepare lessons is the ideal situation your school should be aiming for. However, class teachers have somewhat less control than SLT over the top-level decisions that can make this a reality. Furthermore, teachers will be as aware as SLT of the implications of using the goodwill of their TA(s) to create meeting times – maybe more so. In our experience, it is likely to take some time (two or three terms) for a school to reach a position when all TAs have meeting time with teachers. So, what can teachers do in the short term to make the most of the brief time they have with TAs?

Firstly, ensure TAs receive lesson plans as far in advance as possible. Sharing plans early allows TAs to get back to teachers with any queries. Plans are not only the primary mechanism for communicating lesson aims, but also the shared basis on which teachers and TAs can have conversations – even if (as is often the case) this is briefly at the start of the lesson. Where TAs receive plans in advance, they are able to work through what they do and do not understand. This way, conversations are limited to clarifying anything the TA is unclear about, rather than running through, from the top, things they already know.

Secondly, changes to lesson plans are inevitable at times, and this is to be encouraged as good teachers deviate from their plan when they realise it is not working or when they realise a better strategy is required. Teachers should ensure they alert TAs to any changes to their original plan if, for example, assessments from the previous lesson suggest a different approach is needed in the following lesson than that already shared with the TA. Such tweaks will be easier to convey once TAs have an awareness of the overall aim and content of the lesson. The situation to avoid is TAs finding themselves persisting with a particular strategy the teacher has rejected in favour of something more appropriate. This is not an uncommon experience of many TAs who are fortunate to see plans prior to lessons.

Case study

Using teachers' plans to identify where guidance was needed

One secondary school TA used the teacher's long-term plans to see which science topics and lessons were coming up. She was able to identify early on any gaps in her knowledge. The teacher said how useful it was for him to know the limitations of the TA's knowledge, and he took responsibility for explaining trickier concepts to individual pupils, rather than expecting or assuming that the TA would be able to do it.

In the EDTA project, we found that there were positive effects of improving the quality of lesson plans and sharing them with TAs prior to lessons. However, in order to give some flavour of the profound change that is possible, here are two comments from a TA and teacher pair:

> I think with [teacher] sharing the lesson plans ... I'm just noticing I feel more confident with the way I deal with the pupils, because I feel more secure in what I'm expected to do. Sometimes you know, occasionally when you come in cold, you feel unsure and you don't know what to say to the children so much ... So I think sharing the learning objectives and what needs to be achieved and who to focus on, just means I'm much more aware of where to be.
>
> (Primary TA)

I think the benefits outweigh any extra work ... I think to start with, it's a short-term steep learning curve, and then when you actually see the benefit and you think, 'how could I ever go back?' No way. I couldn't at all actually.

(Primary teacher)

Preparation for TAs who lead classes

Our research has shown the quality of lesson planning and information sharing prior to lessons is a key factor in whether lessons covered by TAs and cover supervisors run smoothly and pupils achieve. The DISS project found many teachers avoided planning demanding lessons for planned absences – which is somewhat understandable given the expertise required to deliver them – and instead supplied pupils with 'busy work'.

But under-stimulating work increased the incidences of off-task and disruptive behaviour, which was in any event a challenge for TAs to deal with because the pupils were very aware the person in charge was someone they perceived to have less authority than a teacher. For teachers, the irony is that time saved by not properly planning for absence can be lost by having to follow up behaviour incidents on their return to school.

To protect TAs and cover supervisors, and to ensure as far as possible good classroom work and behaviour in teachers' absence, school leaders must address preparation for lesson cover and build it into the school's policies. TAs and cover supervisors should not be sold short by inadequately planned lessons. You will need to decide the appropriate lesson format and tasks that teachers should be required to provide for TAs covering planned absences.

For more obvious reasons, an unplanned absence is not so easy to prepare for on a day-to-day basis; nevertheless you must consider how you will handle this as a school. Again, the role of the TA covering the lesson and the lesson content should be consistent with the expectations set out in the school policy, so the lessons run as smoothly as possible and are productive.

Heads of year or subject departments could consider building a bank of activities suitable for cover lessons. These lessons should require little specialist knowledge or teaching. These could be group-based activities, which give pupils the opportunity to work together with minimal adult support.

TEACHER-LEVEL DECISIONS

Many teachers will have been asked to cover a lesson at very short notice. If this has ever happened to you, the chances are that in your mind you breathed a sigh a relief when you were told the lesson you had to cover was in a subject you were familiar with and/or with a class you knew well. If, when you arrived in the classroom, there was a thinly written lesson plan or no plan at all, your familiarity with the pupils is likely to have helped the lesson run smoothly and/or your subject knowledge sufficient to ensure they learned and produced some work worth marking.

If the lesson was in a subject and with a class you were not so familiar with, at the very least the lesson was likely to have been largely incident free because, from the pupils' point of view, having a teacher cover the lesson is a signal to them that there is to be no slippage from the expected standards of behaviour.

TAs and cover supervisors tend not to enter cover lessons with the same levels of authority or subject knowledge as teachers. The majority of teachers would not knowingly put a colleague in a situation where they felt they were 'entering the lion's den', yet this can be the experience of many TAs and cover supervisors.

Teachers should ensure that lesson plans are annotated with specific instructions, or even written afresh with the TA in mind. They should ensure the covering TA is aware of where to find resources. Think of any circumstances that could occur for which the TA would need to be ready; leave nothing to chance! If it is possible for teachers to know in advance which TA will be taking their lesson, seek them out and brief them on the lesson plan. Let them know about the needs of particular pupils (for example, those who might need an extra explanation or who are likely to be unsettled by the lesson being led by someone else). One advantage of having subject-based TAs in secondary schools is that there is a familiar and knowledgeable person available for lesson cover and increased opportunities to liaise at short notice.

Key recommendations on the day-to-day preparedness of TAs

- Schools should make whatever adjustments are possible to suit the implementation of effective models of preparation, including adjusting TAs' working hours.
- Look for creative ways to timetable periods in the school day for teacher–TA liaison.
- Formalise the way teachers plan and share information about lessons by instituting a school-wide lesson plan template and process for communication.
- Ensure teachers provide TAs with 'need to know' information for each lesson: be clear about the role TAs are to take; which pupils to support; what tasks to support; and what the expected outcomes are. Share lesson plans prior to lessons and use time before lessons to discuss amendments.
- Encourage teachers to use their whole-class delivery to supplement, model and make explicit strategies, techniques or key vocabulary on the lesson plan.
- Set standards for what teachers must do to ensure TAs are properly prepared to cover lessons in their absence. Have clear expectations of what lesson plans must include. Keep this under review.

Obtaining quality feedback from TAs

Feedback from TAs on the engagement and progress of pupils completes the preparation loop. Feedback is a way of gathering vital information about pupils' incremental learning and development to inform teachers' understanding and interpretation of their work and behaviour, and in turn, inform future lesson planning. Performed correctly, feedback from TAs is also a form of evaluating teachers' deployment decisions; in other words, did the way they used the TA in the lesson produce the planned learning outcomes, and if not, why?

TAs require a clear sense of what constitutes relevant and useful feedback. The evidence is clear that without this, TAs will drift towards providing support and feedback relating to task completion. TAs are not trained teachers: not only have they not had the requisite training on what constitutes quality feedback, but they do not have the responsibility for doing anything with the feedback they provide (i.e. using it as the basis for further lesson planning).

TAs require clear guidance to structure the content of feedback to teachers, whether this is in verbal or written form. The lesson plan template could accommodate space for providing feedback.

In terms of pupil engagement and learning, feedback from TAs should be linked to the learning objectives. It should be more developed for responses indicating poor engagement or lack of progress. Teachers will need to know whether the tasks they set were appropriately targeted, clearly defined and/or adequately differentiated, and whether the teaching approach used was appropriate to the task, based on pupils' performance.

Feedback from TAs is necessary for monitoring pupils' understanding of tasks, as well as outcomes. So the feedback process should include a way to determine *why* things do not work out as planned; for example, whether the task the teacher planned was sufficiently differentiated. This extends to curriculum interventions programmes too (see our discussion on interventions in Chapter 4).

Teachers must have a feedback process to enable them to gain valuable insights into how TAs interpret the tasks given to them, and which can be used to address any misunderstandings or limitations in their perceptions of the work. Similarly, feedback should provide a check and balance for confirming TAs' understanding of lesson content.

TEACHER-LEVEL DECISIONS

TAs have a privileged position within the classroom. They are present at the moment learning happens. That said, learning is not something we can see directly, but we *can* observe its effects in the form of pupils' performance; that is, in the things they say and the work they produce. It is this detailed information on pupils' performance that teachers need in order to inform their planning and teaching. Quality feedback helps teachers to do their job more effectively, and the more rich and informed the feedback is, the better the teaching. And of course, when teaching improves, so does pupils' performance.

In *The Teaching Assistants Guide to Effective Interaction* (2016), Paula Bosanquet, Julie Radford and Rob Webster explore how TAs can provide the valuable feedback that is the fuel for better teaching. They set out a role for TAs as collectors of accurate and detailed feedback *of* learning for the teacher to use in assessment *for* learning. This feedback, which is captured as pupils work, concerns the level of independence with which pupils undertake tasks, and the type and amount of scaffolding they require. The role described for TAs is consistent with our view expressed in the previous chapter, that there is great potential in using TAs in ways to support schools' broader aim of developing pupils' capacity and confidence to take greater ownership over their learning.

Crucial to capturing quality feedback, however, is teachers' understanding that the feedback TAs' record relates to the *processes* pupils follow to achieve the task, not whether they produce the final product. This being the case, teachers need to think in terms of planning tasks for pupils with process success criteria (i.e. what can pupils do?), not product success criteria (i.e. what have they done?).

Teachers in the EDTA project found that feedback was most effective when TAs had been given clear directions from teachers on what they wanted them to feed back, and when feedback was linked to lesson objectives. As our colleagues found, feeding back verbally is quicker than in writing, but the latter is more reliable. Information exchanged swiftly and briefly during a busy lesson changeover is unlikely to contain the level of detail required for effective teacher assessment and lesson planning; plus it is contingent on both the TA and the teacher remembering all the information fit to share.

Teachers we have worked with, including those in the EDTA project, include a designated space on their lesson plans for TAs to provide feedback, but as we have been stressing, there must be some structure or guidance for their comments. There are things teachers will want to know about how the pupils (and the TA) got on, so a framework for feedback can really help. The chapter on providing feedback in *The Teaching Assistant's Guide to Effective Interaction* contains an example of a framework based around the scaffolding role explained in the book.

Case studies

Written forms of feedback 1

TAs in one school received training from the deputy head on assessment of pupils' progress within a lesson and on giving feedback. The school introduced feedback sheets for TAs to complete for the group they worked with, which described the lesson objective, a brief description of the activity and a space to make comments about each pupil. The completed sheets were stuck in the pupils' workbooks as a record of progress and used for planning next steps.

Written forms of feedback 2

One primary school introduced a feedback process using sticky notes and purple pens. If, during lessons, TAs noticed a particularly strong response from a pupil, or a pupil was showing signs of finding something difficult, they would note it down on a sticky note and give it to the teacher before the end of the lesson. This ensured teachers had 'real time' information about how pupils had performed, and which informed their plenary talk.

TAs used their purple pens to mark work. If they had given verbal feedback to a pupil, they marked their work at the point of feedback with a (VF). They also marked some of the work their group had produced, where the answers were straightforward (e.g. right or wrong), and informed the teacher if any pupils struggled.

The deputy headteacher said: 'TAs are all now involved in the on-going assessment of our pupils. They feel they have a valid contribution to make, and have a better understanding of all of the pupils in their class, and now, where possible, meet with parents at parents' evening and contribute to review meetings for pupls with SEN.'

> **Written forms of feedback 3**
>
> Teachers in one primary school developed a shorthand system for using in pupils' books. As one teacher explained: 'A full triangle [means] ... that they could do it all independently, by themselves; [TA] didn't need to really support them. Two sides [∧] means they needed a little bit of support to get going, but they've grasped it; they just need to build their confidence. And one side [/] means they need a lot of support; they can't do this by themselves.'

Feedback from TAs necessarily arrives in summary form, but the value for teachers lies in the how this can be used to inform their further lesson planning.

> If [TA] has worked with a certain group ... She'll assess [their work] and focus [feedback]. She'll tick which part's right ... and then she'll have a discussion with me and I'll say 'How did your group get on?', and she'll pinpoint kids who didn't get to it, or the ones that did and need reinforcement. And then I'll be able to see that as well from her marking.
>
> (Primary teacher)

Key recommendations on obtaining quality feedback from TAs

- Teachers: be specific about what feedback is needed from TAs. Provide focus using a framework, especially if time is tight.
- Try to ensure written feedback is supplemented with some brief discussion.
- Use the structured feedback from TAs to inform future lesson planning. Have a clear sense of what TAs should be doing at each point of the planning, teaching and feedback/assessment cycle.

Summary

It is useful to end here with a brief summary of the conditions schools we have worked with have put in place in order to successfully address the key issues raised in the DISS project concerning TAs' training and day-to-day preparation:

- When creating time for teachers and TAs to meet is regarded as an essential prerequisite of successful classroom collaboration, there is less risk of TAs' interactions with pupils being driven by guesswork and erroneous assumptions.
- Reconfiguring TAs' hours of work is the surest way to creating teacher–TA liaison time.
- When teachers improve the quality and clarity of their lesson plans, instances of TAs going into lessons blind, or relying on picking up information via teachers' whole-class delivery, are reduced.

Chapter 7

Conclusions

In this final short chapter we sum up with some general conclusions about the impact of conducting the MITA process and carrying out the suggestions outlined in this book, based on the experiences of schools we have worked with. First we summarise the main findings from the Effective Deployment of TAs project and then describe some of the key messages to arise from an evaluation of the MITA programme at the UCL Institute of Education (IOE).

Summary of the Effective Deployment of Teaching Assistants (EDTA) project

The starting point for the EDTA project was the startling results on pupil progress from the Deployment and Impact of Support Staff (DISS) project, which additionally showed how TAs commonly have a frontline pedagogical role – but an ineffective one. Problems emerge particularly when TAs are given an ill-defined, informal, instructional role. Furthermore, as the findings from our 2012 Making a Statement (MAST) study revealed, the prevalence and effect of these arrangements are exacerbated for pupils with high-level SEN, who receive the highest amounts of TA support.

We concluded the impact and practice of TAs must be seen in terms of decisions made *about* TAs by school leaders and teachers, not in terms of decisions made *by* TAs. We therefore called for a fundamental reassessment of the way TAs are used in schools.

The aim of the EDTA project (2010–11) was to develop alternative strategies to the three main components of the Wider Pedagogical Role (WPR) model we used to explain the DISS project findings: TA deployment, practice and preparedness. The national, large-scale research project, followed by a coherent and empirically sound explanatory model, was used as the basis for a collaboration with schools on the development of key recommendations.

In the EDTA project, we found there was a good deal of productive work over the school year in relation to all three components of the WPR model. With regard to *deployment*, at the school level, SLTs thought more strategically about the purpose of the TA role and expectations in terms of pupil outcomes. Many conducted an audit of current practices to establish the need for, and the extent of, change required. Overall, attention had been turned to how TAs could 'add value' to the teacher's role, rather than replace it.

Schools formalised new models of TA deployment and implemented wider changes for the following school year. In some schools, TAs were used as 'advocates for change', selling the benefits of doing things differently to the wider staff. Overall, schools had challenged entrenched, unhelpful mindsets towards the use of TAs and provision for pupils with SEN.

There were also marked and productive changes to the deployment of TAs at the classroom level. TAs worked more often with average-attaining and higher-attaining pupils, and teachers spent more time with lower-attaining pupils and those with SEN. This greatly improved and enriched teachers' understanding of these pupils and their needs. Careful thought had been given to less productive uses of TAs; for example, teachers reduced the proportion of time in which TAs were passive during lessons, and TAs more often remained in the classroom with the pupils they supported, thus reducing separation. In line with recommendations by Michael Giangreco and colleagues (2004, 2011), attention had also been given to alternatives to adult support, for example, using peer supports and collaborative group work, and teaching pupils self-help strategies.

With regard to *practice*, there was good work on changing TAs' talk with pupils. This included encouraging TAs to consider when *not* to talk, thereby giving pupils time to respond. Perhaps for the first time, TAs were encouraged to adopt the pedagogical goal that interactions with pupils should be about understanding, *not* task completion. TA practice developed to support formative assessment and initiatives designed to develop the 'softer' sides of learning. Schools worked on two key developments: (i) questioning frameworks to help pupils remain in charge of, and responsible for, their own learning; (ii) strategies to help pupils become independent learners, thereby reducing dependency on adult support.

Finally, in terms of *preparedness*, schools found creating time for teachers and TAs to meet had a positive effect. Primary schools created liaison time by changing TAs' hours of work, though this was still a challenge for secondary schools. The quality and clarity of teachers' lesson plans improved and plans were shared with TAs and supplemented with daily discussion, which made explicit the role and tasks of the TA for each lesson. Involvement in the project also encouraged many schools to instigate performance management processes for TAs.

Overall, we found that engaging in the EDTA project was professionally important for all staff. Teachers became more aware of their responsibilities to pupils and TAs, and it was clear the TAs who took part felt more valued, appreciated and more confident in their role and abilities.

Summary of the Maximising the Impact of Teaching Assistants (MITA) programme

The outcomes of the EDTA project were the basis for the first edition of this book, which in turn established the principles and processes for the MITA programme. At the time of writing (summer 2015), over 70 schools have been involved with the MITA programme at the IOE, since its inception in January 2014. A further 11 schools have completed a parallel course run in collaboration with Essex County Council. All of this work is on-going and growing!

Our evaluation of the first cohorts of schools to complete the IOE course (January to July 2014), based on feedback from participants, found that despite starting from different points, all schools made progress towards understanding and addressing the complex issues of rethinking the TA role and raising the profile of TAs within their school.

School leaders told us a strength of the MITA programme is the way it is structured around a robust evidence-informed organisational framework for decision-making and action, based on extensive empirical research. Our WPR framework helped school leaders appreciate the need for the deep structural change that the research revealed is essential if TAs are to have a lasting and meaningful impact on pupil outcomes.

The programme has helped school leaders think more broadly about the issues relating to TA deployment, preparedness and their interactions with pupils (to some, 'the MITA trinity!'). While training for TAs tends to be quickly identified as an area for attention, on its own, it is no silver bullet. For example, our partner schools recognised that the need for change in relation to improving provision for pupils with SEN extended beyond TAs to improving teachers' practice. Indeed, the incoming SEN Code of Practice proved to be a powerful additional catalyst for change – which was no coincidence. One of the key aims of the MITA programme and book is, as the Code supports, to encourage schools to develop a role for TAs that breaks away from the so-called 'Velcro' model of support for pupils with SEN.

Instead, schools explored the enormous potential of using TAs to help *all* pupils develop the essential skills that underpin successful learning, such as the ability to scaffold their own learning and ask the questions that help them to get better at getting better at learning.

It is worth noting Paula Bosanquet's (University of East London) collaboration with schools in Essex has taken the work on TA–pupil interactions to a new level, and forms the basis for the practical, classroom-tested strategies in our sister book, *The Teaching Assistant's Guide to Effective Interaction* (Bosanquet, Radford and Webster 2016).

Final comment

A constant refrain in this book has been this: in order to bring about the necessary change, it is important that leadership comes from the headteacher. It is not enough, as some school leaders have assumed, to assign the job of reform to the SENCo or another member of staff, especially if they are not members of the SLT.

This conclusion about affecting change is hardly unique. A raft of research attests to why headteachers must drive, not dodge, school workforce issues. School leaders participating in the MITA programme have been driven by a desire to ensure TAs' contribution to school life seriously counts, *as well as* a need to understand why pupils targeted for TA support are negatively affected by the very intervention designed to help them, and how to reverse this situation.

Changing how schools use TAs – from envisioning a blueprint, to gaining consensus, to working in ways consistent with the vision – is necessarily a leadership issue. These, we think, are the 'active ingredients' in producing practices that last and, crucially, pay off in terms of improving pupil outcomes.

We have been delighted with the positive response to the first edition of this book. We have heard from many school leaders and teachers (via email and by meeting them at various conferences and events across the UK) who have told us how they have risen to the challenge of doing something positive and transformative for their TA workforce. We have been fortunate to share some of their stories and experiences in this second edition.

Gratifyingly for us – but moreover the schools – the effort is paying off, as they begin to see the benefits of addressing the key challenge of defining the role, purpose and contribution of TAs within their setting.

In terms of policy, successive governments have been inactive on the issues raised by the DISS project (2009); though in truth, this inertia dates back much further. In some senses, it matters less in the current educational context, because encouragingly, schools appear to be seizing the initiative and using the freedoms they have been given to set the agenda. It is still early days, but empowering school leaders in this way might potentially have an even greater payoff.

As the statistics show, no jurisdiction in the world has gone as far as the UK in its use of teaching assistants. If we are to realise the treasured aim of keeping pace with international education systems, their contribution will be essential. With a growing number of schools starting to set the pace, the prize awaiting the UK is to become a world leader in this area.

Appendices

Appendix 1 Sorting activity

Instructions: Get teachers and TAs to work through the statements below and decide if each task is something TAs should do, may sometimes do, or should not be expected to do.

	Should do	Sometimes do	Not expected to do
TAs should always be assigned to a group of pupils in a lesson.			
TAs should ask questions to the whole class at times.			
TAs should attend meetings with parents/carers.			
TAs should be involved in the planning process.			
TAs should be responsible for individual education plans.			
TAs should be responsible for the displays in the classroom.			
TAs should be used to support the range of pupils within the class.			
TAs should check reading records.			
TAs should deliver interventions.			
TAs should do photocopying.			
TAs should encourage pupils to take responsibility for their own learning.			
TAs should ensure the classroom is tidy at the end of the day.			
TAs should get resources ready for lessons.			
TAs should give pupils attention in a way that balances the needs of individuals and the group as a whole.			
TAs should introduce the lesson starter.			
TAs should make assessment judgements about the pupils they work with.			
TAs should mark tests.			
TAs should mark work for the group they have worked with.			
TAs should plan and prepare activities for the group they work with.			
TAs should provide feedback to pupils on their progress.			
TAs should provide regular feedback to the teacher.			
TAs should reinforce the teacher's instructions.			
TAs should support the behaviour management of the class within a lesson.			
TAs should team teach alongside the teacher.			

Appendix 2 Action plan template

For each action plan point, rate the effectiveness of current practice: 1 = all/almost all practice is ineffective; 2 = mainly ineffective practice, but with some features of good practice; 3 = good practice in evidence, but needs to be more consistently applied throughout the school; 4 = mainly good practice, but some improvement required; 5 = all/almost all practice is effective.

Action plan point	Steps we will take	Predicted timescale	Staff and resources (specify lead member of staff)	Potential issues we might face	Success criteria	Monitoring (how we will measure progress)
Deployment (e.g. Defining TAs' role/purpose; classroom organisation; support for SEN) 1 2 3 4 5						
Teacher/school-level action (e.g. Teachers' role in class; provision for high-level SEN) 1 2 3 4 5						
Practice (e.g. Developing a teaching and learning identity for TAs; effective interactions; developing independence) 1 2 3 4 5						
Teacher/school-level action (e.g. Training required) 1 2 3 4 5						
Preparedness (e.g. Creating liaison time for teachers and TAs; improving pre/post lesson communication; training) 1 2 3 4 5						
Teacher/school-level action (e.g. improving lesson planning; managing interventions; teacher training) 1 2 3 4 5						

Appendix 3 TA policy agreement

-- NAME OF SCHOOL --

Our Agreement on the Use of Teaching Assistants

TAs can expect the senior leadership team to:

- Ensure each TA is deployed in a role that reflects their skills and aptitudes.
- Define, clearly and properly, the tasks and duties each TA can expect to be asked to perform in their role, and specify their contribution to teaching and learning at [name of school].
- Provide timely and appropriate training and preparation to ensure TAs are confident and ready to undertake the tasks they are given.
- Avoid deploying TAs in roles for which they are not specifically trained or that are more appropriately undertaken by a qualified teacher. (Some very exceptional circumstances may apply.)
- Recognise and celebrate TAs' contribution to teaching and learning, and treat them as professionals in their own right.
- Provide induction and professional development opportunities, supervision and performance reviews commensurate with maintaining their professional identity.
- Ensure teaching staff are aware of their role and responsibility for ensuring TAs are deployed appropriately and are properly prepared for the tasks they give them.
- Train and support teachers to ensure they have the skills and knowledge to deploy TAs appropriately and consistently.

TAs can expect teachers to:

- Be aware of the school's expectations of how to deploy and prepare TAs, and ensure their contribution to teaching and learning is consistent with our whole school aims.
- Know the respective roles and skills of the TAs they work with most frequently and deploy them appropriately.
- Communicate adequate information and instructions about lessons ahead of time, and clearly specify TAs' role in, and contribution, to each lesson.
- Provide opportunities for TAs to feed back after lessons and provide clear guidance on what information should be fed back.
- Respond in a positive and timely fashion to requests from TAs for information about lessons, pupils, curriculum content, instructional techniques or any other information essential to ensuring their effective deployment in lessons and contribution to learning.
- Discharge responsibilities to TAs that, as the lead professional in the classroom, belong to them.
- Recognise and reinforce TAs' professional identity and their status within the school.
- Contribute to induction and training, supervision and performance reviews for TAs.
- Request training and guidance in order to ensure they have the skills and knowledge to meet their professional duties and responsibilities as a teacher, in relation to deploying TAs appropriately.

The senior leadership team and teachers expect TAs to:

- Act in a manner that upholds the professional identity of TAs at [name of school].
- Participate in the school's induction programme and performance review process.
- Make the most of training and professional development opportunities to develop their knowledge and skills.
- Prompt teachers for pre-lesson information and to ask for clarification where required.
- Perform and interact with pupils in ways that are consistent with what the school expects from TAs in terms of their contribution to teaching and learning.
- Contribute to lesson planning and feedback at teachers' request.

Appendix 4 Questions and key words for critical thinking

Are you sure? How do you know? Can you tell me why?

Remembering	Understanding	Applying	Analysing	Evaluating	Creating
You want to find out what the child knows.	*You want to find out what the child understands.*	*You want to support the child in solving a problem, using what has been learned.*	*You want to support the child to examine and break down information into parts.*	*You want to support the child in reflecting on and evaluating work and ideas.*	*You want to support the child to represent information in a new or alternative way.*
Who ...?	Tell me in your own words ...	How would you solve ... using what you've learned ...?	What are the parts or features of ...?	What works/worked well?	What changes would you make to solve ...?
What ...?	Which is the best answer, and why?	What do you know already that could help you?	What is the theme ...?	What would you change?	Can you think of another way?
Where ...?	What facts and ideas show ...?	What other way would you plan to ...?	How is ... related to ...?	How could it be improved?	Can you predict/estimate?
When ...?	How are these the same? Different?	What would happen if ...?	How could you sort these?	Do you agree with the actions ...? with the outcome ...?	What do you think it's going to be?
Which ...?	What is the effect of ...?	What do you think you need to do next?	Why do you think ...?	What is your opinion of ...?	How would you adapt ... to create a different ...?
Why ...?	What is the main idea of ...?	How could you use what you have learned?	What evidence can you find to support this?	What information would you use to support these views?	How could you put all your ideas together?
How would you show/explain/ describe ...?	What does this mean?		What conclusions can you draw ...?	How would you prove ...? disprove ...?	
			What is the function of ...?	What/which is the most important ... and why?	
				Why did they choose ...? How would you do it differently?	

Appendix 5 Prompts for facilitating learning and thinking

These prompts will help you to *facilitate* pupils' *learning* and *thinking* in lessons.

Remember: '*Telling them the answer is not always learning.*'

- Show me something that is solid.
- Can you tell me the equipment you have used?
- Find something that is used to make an electrical circuit.
- Having read the information, what is it telling you?
- Where can you find the meaning of the word?
- What does ... mean? Why has this happened?
- What could you say about ...?
- What might happen next? What do you see? How do you know?
- What is in the picture? Which ... go together?
- Can you explain? Are you sure this is true? How do you know?
- Where did you get the information from?
- How are you going to present the results?
- Explain the meaning of two key words.
- What have you learnt about ... today?

- *Have you given pupils time to answer the question?*
- *Are you allowing the pupils to work independently?*
- *Are you encouraging pupils to work in pairs or groups?*

References

Alborz, A., Pearson, D., Farrell, P. and Howes, A. (2009) *The Impact of Adult Support Staff on Pupils and Mainstream Schools*. London: Department for Children, Schools and Families and Institute of Education.

Anderson, V. and Finney, M. (2008) '"I'm a TA not a PA!": Teaching assistants working with teachers', in G. Richards and F. Armstrong (eds) *Key Issues for Teaching Assistants: Working in Diverse and Inclusive Classrooms*, pp.73–83. Oxon: Routledge.

Bach, S., Kessler, I. and Heron, P. (2004) 'Support roles and changing job boundaries in the public services: The case of teaching assistants in British primary schools'. Paper presented at *International Labour Process Conference*, Amsterdam, April.

Baines, E., Blatchford, P. and Kutnick, P. (2008) *Promoting Effective Group Work in the Primary Classroom: A Handbook for Teachers and Practitioners*. Oxon: Routledge.

Beer, M. and Nohria, N. (2000) 'Cracking the code of change', *Harvard Business Review*, 78 (3): 133–141.

Blatchford, P., Bassett, P., Brown, P., Martin, C., Russell, A. and Webster, R. with Babayigit, S. and Haywood, N. (2008) *The Deployment and Impact of Support Staff in Schools and the Impact of the National Agreement: Results from Strand 2 Wave 1 – 2005/06*. London: Department for Children, Schools and Families.

Blatchford, P., Russell, A., Bassett, P., Brown, P. and Martin, C. (2004) *The Effects and Role of Teaching Assistants in English Primary Schools (Years 4 to 6) 2000–2003: Results from the Class Size and Pupil-Adult Ratios (CSPAR) Project. Final Report*. London: Department for Education and Skills.

Blatchford, P., Webster, R. and Russell, A. (2012a) *Challenging the Role and Deployment of Teaching Assistants in Mainstream Schools: The Impact on Schools. Final Report on the Effective Deployment of Teaching Assistants (EDTA) Project*. Available online at: http://maximisingtas.co.uk/assets/content/edtareport-2.pdf (accessed 10.04.15).

Blatchford, P., Russell, A. and Webster, R. (2012b) *Reassessing the Impact of Teaching Assistants: How Research Challenges Practice and Policy*. Oxon: Routledge.

Bosanquet, P., Radford. J. and Webster, R. (2016) *The Teaching Assistant's Guide To Effective Interaction: How to Maximise Your Impact*. Oxon: Routledge.

Brown, J. and Harris, A. (2010) *Increased Expenditure on Associate Staff in Schools and Changes in Student Attainment*. London: Training and Development Agency for Schools.

Caudrey, A. (1985) 'Growing role of parents in class causes alarm', *Times Educational Supplement*, 12th April, p.1 (Issue no. 3589).

Curliss, A. (2014) 'Berger: NC pay raise is more important than teacher assistants', *News and Observer*, 7th June 2014. Available online at: www.ncspin.com/berger-nc-pay-raise-is-more-important-than-teacher-assistants/ (accessed 02.04.15).

Department for Education (2012) *Local Authority and School Expenditure on Education, Children's Services and Social Care For 2010–11, Including School Revenue Balances (OSR 03/2012)*. London: Department for Education.

Department for Education [educationgovuk] (2014) Interview with Nicky Morgan. Uploaded to *YouTube* on 4 September. Available online at: www.youtube.com/watch?v=sKk_6Kr6qyk (accessed 29.10.14).

Department for Education (2015) *School Workforce in England: November 2014*. Published on 2 July 2015. Available online at: www.gov.uk/government/statistics/school-workforce-in-england-november-2014 (accessed 03.08.15).

Department for Education and Department of Health (2015) *Special Educational Needs and Disability Code of Practice: 0 to 25 Years. Statutory Guidance for Organisations Which Work With and Support Children and Young People Who Have Special Educational Needs or Disabilities*. January 2015. Available online at: www.gov.uk/government/uploads/system/uploads/attachment_data/file/398815/SEND_Code_of_Practice_January_2015.pdf (accessed 09.04.15).

Department for Education and Skills (2003) *Raising Standards and Tackling Workload: A National Agreement*. London: Department for Education and Skills.

Dunne, L., Goddard, G. and Woodhouse, C. (2008) 'Teaching assistants' perceptions of their professional role and their experiences of doing a foundation degree', *Improving Schools*, 11 (3): 239–249.

Ekins, A. (2015) *The Changing Face of Special Educational Needs: Impact and Implications for SENCos and their Schools*. Second Edition. Oxon: Routledge.

Farrell, P., Alborz, A., Howes, A. and Pearson, D. (2010) 'The impact of teaching assistants on improving pupils' academic achievement in mainstream schools: a review of the literature', *Educational Review*, 62 (4): 435–448.

Finn, J.D., Gerber, S.B., Farber, S.L. and Achilles, C.M. (2000) 'Teacher aides: an alternative to small classes?', in M. C. Wang and J. D. Finn (eds) *How Small Classes Help Teachers Do their Best*, pp.131–174. Philadelphia, PA: Temple University Center for Research in Human Development.

Fraser, C. and Meadows, S. (2008) 'Children's views of teaching assistants in primary schools', *Education 3–13*, 36 (4): 351–363.

Friswell, J. (2013) 'The SEN Code of Practice explained', *SecEd*. Available online at: www.sec-ed.co.uk/best-practice/the-sen-code-of-practice-explained (accessed 29.10.14).

Gerber, S.B., Finn, J.D., Achilles, C.M. and Boyd-Zacharias, J. (2001) 'Teacher aides and students' academic achievement', *Educational Evaluation and Policy Analysis*, 23 (2): 123–143.

Giangreco, M.F. (2003) 'Working with paraprofessionals', *Educational Leadership*, 61 (2): 50–53.

Giangreco, M.F. (2010) 'One-to-one paraprofessionals for students with disabilities in inclusive classrooms: is conventional wisdom wrong?' *Intellectual and Developmental Disabilities*, (48): 1–13.

Giangreco, M.F. and Broer, S.M. (2005) 'Questionable utilization of paraprofessionals in inclusive schools: are we addressing symptoms or causes?' *Focus on Autism and Other Developmental Disabilities*, 20: 10–26.

Giangreco, M.F., Broer, S.M. and Suter, J.C. (2011) 'Guidelines for selecting alternatives to overreliance on paraprofessionals: field-testing in inclusion-oriented schools', *Remedial and Special Education*, 32 (1): 22-38.

Giangreco, M.F., Doyle, M.B. and Suter, J.C. (2014) 'Teacher assistants in inclusive classrooms', in L. Florian (ed.), *The SAGE Handbook of Special Education, Second Edition*, pp. 429-439, London: SAGE.

Giangreco, M.F., Halvorsen, A., Doyle, M.B. and Broer, S.M. (2004) 'Alternatives to overreliance on paraprofessionals in inclusive schools', *Journal of Special Education Leadership*, 17 (2): 82–90.

Giangreco, M.F., Yuan, S., McKenzie, B., Cameron, P. and Fialka, J. (2005) '"Be careful what you wish for …": Five reasons to be concerned about the assignment of individual paraprofessionals', *Teaching Exceptional Children*, 37(5): 28–34.

Gross, J. (2015) *Beating Bureaucracy in Special Educational Needs*. Third Edition. Oxon: Routledge.

Hansard (2014) House of Commons debate, 18 March, col 227WH.

Higgins, S., Katsipataki, M., Kokotsaki, D., Coleman, R., Major, L.E. and Coe, R. (2013) *The Sutton Trust-Education Endowment Foundation Teaching and Learning Toolkit*. London: Education Endowment Foundation. Available online at: http://educationendowment foundation.org.uk/uploads/pdf/Teaching_Assistants_Toolkit_References.pdf (accessed 02.04.15).

Knoster, T., Villa R. and Thousand, J. (2000) 'A framework for thinking about systems change', in R. Villa and J. Thousand (eds), *Restructuring for Caring and Effective Education: Piecing the Puzzle Together*, pp. 93–128. Baltimore: Paul H. Brookes Publishing Co.

Kotter, J.P. (1995) Leading change: Why transformation efforts fail, *Harvard Business Review*, 73 (2): 59–67.

Kotter, J.P. (1996) *Leading Change*. Harvard: Harvard Business School Press.

Lamb, B. (2009) *The Lamb Inquiry: Special Educational Needs and Parental Confidence*. London: Department for Children, Schools and Families.

Muijs, R.D. and Reynolds, D. (2001) *Effective Teaching: Evidence and Practice*. London: Paul Chapman.

Nicoletti, C. and Rabe, B. (2014) *Spending it Wisely: How Can Schools Use Resources to Help Poorer Pupils?* London: Nuffield Foundation.

Norwich, B. and Lewis, A. (2001) 'Mapping a pedagogy for special educational needs', *British Educational Research Journal*, 27 (3): 313–329.

Ofsted (2005) *Managing Challenging Behaviour*. London: Office for Standards in Education.

Ofsted (2015) *School Inspection Handbook – DRAFT* (Ref: 150066). Available online at: www.gov.uk/government/uploads/system/uploads/attachment_data/file/436039/School_inspection_handbook_from_September_2015.pdf (accessed 03.08.15).

Radford, J., Bosanquet, P., Webster, R. and Blatchford. P. (2015) 'Scaffolding learning for independence: Clarifying teacher and TA roles for children with SEN', *Learning and Instruction*, 36 (1): 1–10.

Radford, J., Bosanquet, P., Webster, R., Blatchford. P and Rubie-Davies. C (2014) 'Fostering learner independence through heuristic scaffolding: A valuable role for teaching assistants', *International Journal of Educational Research*, 63 (1): 116–126.

Radford, J., Rubie-Davies, C., Blatchford, P., Russell, A. and Webster, R. (2012) 'The practice of TAs', in Blatchford *et al.* (2012b).

Rubie-Davies, C., Blatchford, P., Webster, R., Koutsoubou, M. and Basset, P. (2010) 'Enhancing student learning? A comparison of teacher and teaching assistant interaction with pupils', *School Effectiveness and School Improvements*, 21 (4): 429–449.

Scottish Government (2011) *Summary Statistics for Schools in Scotland. No.2. 2011 Edition*. Available online at: www.scotland.gov.uk/Publications/2011/12/06114834/0 (accessed 14.05.12).

Sharples, J., Webster, R. and Blatchford, P. (2015) *Making Best Use of Teaching Assistants. Guidance Report. March 2015*. London: Education Endowment Foundation. Available online at: https://educationendowmentfoundation.org.uk/uploads/pdf/Making_best_use_of_TAs_printable.pdf (accessed 02.04.15).

Slavin, R.E., Lake, C., Davis, S. and Madden, N. (2009) *Effective Programs for Struggling Readers: A Best Evidence Synthesis.* Baltimore, MD: Johns Hopkins University, Center for Research and Reform in Education.

Statistics for Wales (2011) *First Release (SDR 153/2011(R)): Schools' Census 2011: Final Results – Revised.* Available online at: http://wales.gov.uk/topics/statistics/headlines/schools2011/110906/?lang=en (accessed 14.05.12).

Thomas, G. (1992) *Effective Classroom Teamwork: Support of Intrusion?* Oxon: Routledge.

Thorpe, L., Trewhitt, K. and Zuccollo, J. (2013) *Must Do Better: Spending on Schools,* London: Reform. Available online at: www.reform.co.uk/resources/0000/0765/Must_do_better_Spending_on_schools.pdf (accessed 02.04.15).

Ward, H. (2014) Teaching assistants do make a difference, *Times Educational Supplement,* 7 February, pp.6–7. Also available online at: www.tes.co.uk/article.aspx?storycode=6400487 (accessed 04.04.15).

Webster, R. (2014a) '2014 Code of Practice: How research evidence on the role and impact of teaching assistants can inform professional practice', *Educational Psychology and Practice,* 30 (3): 232–237.

Webster, R. (2014b) *How Headteachers are Maximising the Impact of Teaching Assistants and Getting Results.* Available online at: https://ioelondonblog.wordpress.com/2014/09/05/how-headteachers-are-maximising-the-impact-of-teaching-assistants-and-getting-results (accessed 28.10.14).

Webster, R. (2015) 'The classroom experiences of pupils with special educational needs in mainstream primary schools – 1976 to 2012. What do data from systematic observation studies reveal about pupils' educational experiences over time?' *British Educational Research Journal,* published online, 9 March 2015. DOI: 10.1002/berg.3181.

Webster, R. and Blatchford, P. (2013) 'The educational experiences of pupils with a Statement for special educational needs in mainstream primary schools. Results from a systematic observation study', *European Journal of Special Needs Education,* 28 (4): 463–479.

Webster, R. and Blatchford, P. (2015) 'Worlds apart? The nature and quality of the educational experiences of pupils with a Statement for special educational needs in mainstream primary schools', *British Educational Research Journal,* 41 (2): 324–342.

Webster, R., Blatchford, P. and Russell, A. (2013) 'Challenging and changing how schools use teaching assistants: Findings from the Effective Deployment of Teaching Assistants project,' *School Leadership and Management,* 33 (1): 78–96.

Webster, R., Blatchford, P., Bassett, P., Brown, P., Martin, C. and Russell, A. (2010) 'Double standards and first principles: Framing teaching assistant support for pupils with special educational needs', *European Journal of Special Educational Needs,* 25 (4): 319–336 .

Wiliam, D. (2010) 'How should we use what we know about learning to read?' Keynote address at *'Changing Lives': 7th International Reading Recovery Institute,* at the UCL Institute of Education, London, 8 July.

Woolf, M. and Griffiths, S. (2013) '230,000 classroom assistants face axe', *The Sunday Times,* 2nd June, p.1 (Issue no. 9847).

Workforce Agreement Monitoring Group (WAMG) (2008) *The Appropriate Deployment of Support Staff in Schools. WAMG Note 22.* London: Workforce Agreement Monitoring Group. Available online at: www.atl.org.uk/Images/WAMG22%20(Deployment%20of%20support%20staff).pdf (accessed 10.04.15).

Index

www.routledge.com/education